"We have implemented Sand... riod of years to successfully grow our business. We have two call centers with over 100 people in each, and these valuable everyday resources have helped us hire the right people, coach them to success, and ensure a motivated team has the right processes to maintain selling at a high level."

—**Scott Cato,** General Manager, AutoAssure

"We first called Sandler for some training for our call-center people, but they brought much more to the table than training. They put a process in place for hiring, coaching, and onboarding the right people and the right sales managers for our call centers. This created not only growth, but a better bottom line with lower turnover and better people."

—**Drew Clancy,** President, Publishing Concepts

"For most people, the very words 'call center' summon up images of a boiler room. That's not the goal. At Axiometrics our inside sales personnel are complete, professional, consultative salespeople—not appointment setters, order takers, or script sellers. Sandler's approach to call-center success simply works. It is much more productive; the number of meaningful conversations and product demonstrations could not be duplicated with an outside sales team. It allows the sales process to be better coached; the coaches are right there as the sale unfolds. It certainly makes the sales day more productive; there's no wondering what your salespeople are really up to. And, so importantly, the Sandler approach saves the prospect's very valuable time."

—**Keith Walters,** Chief Operating Officer, Axiometrics

CALL CENTER SUCCESS
THE SANDLER WAY

Designing and Running a Profitable Inside Sales Call Center

THOMAS NIESEN

Sandler Training

© 2016 Sandler Systems, Inc. All rights reserved.

Reproduction, modification, storage in a retrieval system or retransmission, in any form or by any means, electronic, mechanical, or otherwise, is strictly prohibited without the prior written permission of Sandler Systems, Inc.

S Sandler Training (with design), Sandler, Sandler Submarine (words and design), and Sandler Selling System are registered service marks of Sandler Systems, Inc.

Because the English language lacks a generic singular pronoun that indicates both genders, we have used the masculine pronouns for the sake of style, readability, and brevity. This material applies to both men and women.

Paperback ISBN: 978-0-692-77043-6

E-book ISBN: 978-0-692-77671-1

I would like to dedicate this book to all the clients and friends who took the time to teach me so much about business, sales, and life over the years; to a great and growing team in Lareal and Brisa; and to Sherri, the best business partner and life partner anyone could ask for.

CONTENTS

ACKNOWLEDGMENTS ix

FOREWORD xi

INTRODUCTION xiii

PART ONE: THE SYSTEM

CHAPTER 1: Call-Center Selling: An Overview. 3

CHAPTER 2: Why Traditional Sales Training Doesn't Work . . 17

CHAPTER 3: Communication. 23

CHAPTER 4: More on Bonding & Rapport. 31

CHAPTER 5: The Up-Front Contract 37

CHAPTER 6: Pain 45

CHAPTER 7: Budget. 51

CHAPTER 8: Decision 57

CHAPTER 9: Fulfillment and Post-Sell. 63

PART TWO: THE ENVIRONMENT AND THE PEOPLE

CHAPTER 10: BAT and the Call-Center Environment. 71

CHAPTER 11: Sales Management. 95

CHAPTER 12: A Deeper Dive into Managing
a Call Center 105

CHAPTER 13: Hiring the Right Salespeople
for Your Call Center. .119

PART THREE: THE SCRIPTS

CHAPTER 14: The Scripts 127

PART FOUR: THE ROAD FROM HERE

EPILOGUE. 143

APPENDIX: CASE STUDY

CASE STUDY: PCI 147

ACKNOWLEDGMENTS

I would like to thank all of the people at Sandler® Corporate for putting up with and listening to my ideas, notably: Dave Mattson (who made me a Sandler groupie), Margaret Jacks, Rachel Miller, Mike Montague, Yusuf Toropov, and Jennifer Willard, as well as all of the Sandler partners who have come and gone over the years, who are too numerous to list here. I must also express my gratitude to Lareal, Brisa, Aidan, Sherri, Brandi, and Jimmy for their unyielding support during this project's development. My thanks also go out to Jerry Dorris and Laura Matthews, who provided invaluable help during the editing and production process.

FOREWORD

By every measure, call centers have been surging in popularity. The Bureau of Labor Statistics expects call-center employment to grow 38% over the next five years, a rate nearly twice that of similar occupations. Much of that growth comes from employment of call-center salespeople, which looks to remain strong. Yet the numbers don't always reflect growth from the standpoint of sales efficiency—or perceived levels of service or utility to the prospect/customer.

Too many call-center sales teams are staffed by people using the wrong script and making the wrong offer in the wrong way at the wrong time—annoying consumers and adversely affecting margins. The best current research suggests that, although growth of call centers seems likely to continue, there is also a growing disdain among consumers toward the industry as a whole.

Here's the good news, though. It doesn't have to be that way. Managers can change the call-center paradigm, improve relationships with consumers, and boost margins—all at the same time.

We've spoken to many, many sales managers who've asked us whether we could point them toward a better way—a Sandler way—to manage and grow a call center. They've asked us if we would help them create and support phone discussions that result in more win/win outcomes for both the members of the sales team and the person on the other end of the line. They've asked us whether individual and team productivity truly can be improved dramatically.

The answer to all these questions is an emphatic "yes." Tom Niesen's book—based on his own years of personal experience in transforming call centers—decisively proves that. What follows is a long-overdue call for constructive change within the call-center selling environment. Tom has brought that kind of positive, lasting change to many selling teams. This book can help bring it to yours.

David H. Mattson
President/CEO, Sandler Training

INTRODUCTION

Call Center Success the Sandler Way is the culmination of decades of front-line work with call-center teams in many different specialty areas. However, I have written it in such a way that it focuses only on universal management principles—that is to say, on management principles that I know, from personal experience, are relevant to leaders responsible for any call-center team, operating in any selling environment.

Even so, I know it's quite common for managers and owners to push back against some of the ideas outlined here the first time they encounter them. Many of those ideas may seem unusual to you when you come across them in the pages that follow. You may even be tempted to conclude that the book is not relevant to your industry. My request to you is a simple one: Keep an open mind.

Please do finish reading the book before you make any final decision about whether and how to implement the ideas you encounter here. Also, please do reach out to a Sandler trainer once you have finished *Call Center Success the Sandler Way*, so you can discuss how the principles I share here can be applied to your business. If you are responsible for the performance of a call-center team tasked with selling something, I promise you that what follows is relevant to you.

Thomas Niesen

THE SYSTEM

CHAPTER ONE

Call-Center Selling: An Overview

I wrote this book for people who are responsible for managing call centers and supervising call-center salespeople. In some cases, that includes the owners of the call center.

Typically, the people I work with tell me they are frustrated with high turnover of good potential closers, concerned about low activity or not the right activity, or unhappy with consistently low close ratios throughout the sales floor. If any of that is relevant to your world, this book was written for you.

This first chapter will help you understand the difference between outside selling, inside selling, and call-center selling. If you already have a call center, Chapter 1 will be helpful because it will encourage the habit of defining your center as what it needs to be: a profit center. If you are you thinking about starting a call center, this chapter will give you an introduction to what's unique about call centers and the people you'll need to find to work there.

At various points in the book after this first chapter, I'll be sharing more specific advice on how best to set up and run a more profitable call center. This will come in two forms: suggestions for you as the manager of the center and suggestions that you can share with salespeople.

OUTSIDE, INSIDE, AND CALL-CENTER SELLING

Let's look closely at these three different methods of selling.

Outside Selling

Outside selling is what happens when the salesperson actually has to set up an appointment, get in the car—or perhaps even the plane—and visit a prospect in person. Typically the meeting, which is set up ahead of time, will last something like an hour. If the salesperson is a well-trained professional, the purpose of that meeting is qualification. The salesperson wants to find out whether or not the individual is a qualified prospect. The important thing to remember about outside selling is that it is usually anything but a one-call close. Frequently, the salesperson must go back or do something after-the-fact if the sale is to be secured. Business is seldom concluded on the spot during the first meeting. Sales cycles for the outside-selling salesperson may be relatively short, i.e., a week or less, or they may be very long, i.e., a year or more. It depends on what the person is selling, what the market is doing, and what is likeliest to help the buyer(s) become comfortable enough to make a purchase decision.

Inside Selling

Inside selling is very similar to outside selling, but with the difference that today's advanced communication tools allow the salesperson to close the sale without visiting the prospect in person. Where the outside-selling salesperson sets a meeting at a specific date and time and shows up in person, the inside-selling salesperson might set up a specific date and time for an online video call, an online slide presentation, or a webinar. Twenty years ago, communications technology was not as advanced as it is today, and inside-selling salespeople frequently had to overcome insurmountable obstacles. Now, with meeting tools allowing salespeople to interact with prospects as though they were in the same room, the inside-selling model has gained a lot of traction. Today, there's very little that can be sold by an outside-selling salesperson that can't also be sold by an inside-selling salesperson. One big difference between the two models is that inside selling is far less likely to involve servicing the account once the sale has been closed. In addition, sales cycles for inside selling tend to be somewhat shorter. Another important difference is that extremely high-dollar-value or complex sales generally do not follow this model.

Call-Center Selling

Now we come to **call centers,** which are the focus of this book. This type of selling is not to be confused with outside selling, and, though it is a variation on inside selling, the salespeople involved tend to have very different profiles. In a call-center environment, you have anywhere between three and 300 people in a room, on the phone. Typically, they are either: 1) making outgoing calls on a phone that is set up with an automatic dialer so that shortly after they hang up, the next line on the list rings; or 2) receiving incoming calls that have been generated by some kind of marketing effort. In the first situation, call-center employees might make 200 outgoing calls a day. In the second situation, a call-center representative may field between 100 and 200 calls daily. What's interesting for the call center employee, in stark contrast to the outside-selling salesperson and many inside-selling salespeople, is that these sales typically do conclude in one or two phone calls, with a one-call close being by far the most common sale. In those situations when there is a two-call close, that next call typically takes place within 24 to 48 hours. Compared to the other two selling models, this cycle is lightning speed. In some cases, outbound-call call centers focus on setting up face-to-face appointments for outside-selling salespeople, but this is far less common, and this kind of selling is not the focus of this book.

WHY CALL CENTERS MATTER

Even in this age of "do not call" lists and voicemail jail, more and more companies are setting up call centers to drive new business. Why is that? Well, it could be because people are spending less and less time shopping and more time just buying. Recently, a study showed that as little as ten years ago, the buying process for most people started when they picked up the phone and started to talk to a salesperson, either in person or on the phone. In today's world with all the data at customers' fingertips, a salesperson isn't contacted until the consumer is much closer to making a buying decision.

For many purchases, people don't feel the need to spend a whole lot of time in front of a salesperson—or even much time on the phone. Therefore, it might make more sense to have a call center since, for these purchases, the conversations and fact-finding are taking up a relatively brief span of time. When you target such consumers, though, there are certain questions you'll have to consider. How do you get them to pick up the phone and stay on the line when you call? Or, in an inbound model: How do you get them to dial the phone and contact your call center? Once you have them on the phone, how do you keep them on the phone and turn that phone call into profit?

The Pros

Let's take a look now at the benefits of a call center. The first and most obvious benefit is that the cost of the sale goes down. The cost of an outside-selling salesperson is expensive, not so much in salary but in travel and expenses. In today's world, the cost of financing a single outside-selling salesperson in the United States would typically be in excess of $100,000, while the cost of an inside-selling salesperson might be a quarter of that.

Another advantage is that you have more control over people who are sitting inside a call center all day, either accepting incoming calls you point toward them or engaging with people answering the outgoing calls your system generates. You have a far better measurement of dollars per hour, compared to a loss of control and fewer accurate measurements with people selling outside the office.

A third major advantage is the typical sales manager-to-salesperson ratio is 1:8 in the outside-selling world; in a call center, it is typically about 1:25.

The Cons

Now, how about the downside of call-center selling? There are a lot of factors you'll have to mitigate to make the call center a success.

It takes a special type of employee to sit on the phone all day talking to people who might not be all that friendly, and those employees are pretty hard to find. Although some will stick around, it's more likely there will be high turnover in the call center no matter how good a job you do of hiring, onboarding, and managing. You should expect to be constantly bringing on and constantly losing people—that's just one of the realities of doing business in this arena.

Most of the time, you will be working with people who need to have the entire sales process scripted out for them in advance.

Your salespeople have a very short period of time to make the right impression with the caller.

Your management style is critical. It must be active, not reactive, and it must incorporate an interactive approach that avoids "pushing the buttons" of employees. Developing this kind of management style takes a little practice. You'll learn more about establishing the right management style a little later on in the book, when we talk about transactional analysis, the foundation of the Sandler Selling System® methodology.

Your compensation plan must be as precise and consistent as the sales roadmap you hand your people. Such a plan takes time and attention to develop.

You have to generate sufficient incoming or outgoing call traffic, and that traffic has to be present all the time your center is in operation. If the phones are not ringing or being dialed, you are losing money. It's that simple.

The call-center sales cycle is much faster than in other selling environments, which means that some people will not adapt well to this type of selling. Success in other selling environments does not automatically equate to success in the call-center environment.

In order to put the best practices described in this book into action, you will need to operate a high-tech call center. That probably means you will need to make some investments.

A DEEPER DIVE: FOUR CRITICAL FACTORS FOR CALL-CENTER SUCCESS

There are four critical factors to consider for call-center success.

People

Understand that not all good call-center salespeople look great, dress great, or even care how they look. Some excellent call-center salespeople will give you a terrible first impression, perhaps by the way they dress and the way they look or even the way they act in person. But get them on the phone and give them a way to make money where they don't have to interact face-to-face, and they will surprise you.

Leave your first-impression criticisms at home. Base your decisions on performance, specifically on how the person sounds. Many of our clients have found that applicants who dressed sharp and "looked the part" of a salesperson were the least likely to last more than 30 days in a call-center job.

Management

Successful sales managers for a call center have to have two qualities. They have to know how to coach people in the moment, and they have to be great supervisors of daily, weekly, and monthly metrics. Sales managers who want to take their time and wait a month to look over the numbers will not cut it at a call center. A good call-center manager will never be happy with the status quo and will be looking at data hourly.

Scripts

Scripts are the life blood of a call center and they need to be analyzed, tested, and perfected. Once the right script is found, it must be the path that everyone follows. A change in the script can change the numbers drastically—and quickly. Many managers ask me, "Can we ever go off script?" My answer sounds like this: Going off script only works for the experienced person who has been working with you for a while. This might be someone you allow to experiment. We have often found that veteran salespeople who experiment will watch their own numbers and know quickly if the change from a tested script is worth it or not. You want those salespeople to experiment, and you want them to share the results. Other than that—no. You want your people to stick with the script. (We'll look at what goes into an effective script later on in the book.)

Phone Systems

There are pros and cons to all call-center phone systems today. With today's technology, you can make extraordinary increases in sales efficiency. My advice here, which I will elaborate on as we move forward, is pretty simple: Do not go cheap. Buy the best. A good phone system can help filter out background noise, and, as you will see later on, there should be a lot of background noise to filter out. A good phone system will also let you record and click into any phone conversation, which is essential for the sales manager.

IS THIS FOR YOU?

So, how do you decide whether you should even have a call center?

First, take a look at your sales cycle. Typically a call center is only effective if you have a short cycle or at least a compressed cycle. A call center is also appropriate for a customer service center that is interested in upselling or cross-selling current clients. You might have experienced this firsthand if you have tried to buy something based off a TV commercial. When you called in, you probably noticed that they did their best to sell you several other products or upgrades. They must do this with finesse, of course, so as not to lose the original sale.

Here are some of the other factors to consider in deciding whether this selling model is right for you.

Product Knowledge

What knowledge will your salespeople need to make the sale? If you are looking for technically savvy salespeople or trying to close a highly technical sale that requires a great deal of collaboration among various people on the prospect's side, then a call center isn't for you.

Of course, there has to be some level of knowledge about the product or service, but the main thing to remember is that, at the end of the day, these are time-driven discussions. Look at an outside-selling representative and contrast that person with an inside-selling representative at a call center. You'll find that the things that a salesperson does inside the call center tend to happen much more quickly. That outside-selling representative might take three meetings to establish rapport and might take another three meetings to identify the pain, or problem, to solve. It's different for the person at the call center. Everything must happen within a very short period of time—typically, within just a few minutes. Everything must be condensed, which means there really isn't time for an in-depth technical discussion about the product.

Product/Service

If you're trying to sell something over the phone where the call-center representative has to resolve a number of problems for the prospect before even beginning the sales discussion, call centers may not be the best place to do that.

The reason for that should now be obvious. This is a special kind of selling environment. As you've seen, everything is accelerated. The people working in a call center need to establish rapport fast, set an agenda for the conversation fast, and find the problem fast. Then, if there's a match between what you offer and the problem the caller faces, the representatives need to propose a solution, lock down the sale, and move on.

Customer Base

You don't need a large customer base to get started in call-center selling. Some of the biggest transactions in the call-center world are selling stock trades to customers the salespeople have never met. You can target just about anybody. Just remember that the larger the sale, the more sophisticated and structured your selling process needs to be. Each sales process needs to be broken down in a way that your callers cannot possibly misinterpret as they are executing it.

Profit

How profitable will your call center be? That's one of the questions this book is designed to help you answer. Only you can give the final answer. I will say, though, that we live in an era in which technology can solve all kinds of problems. The correct marketing can make the phone ring.

So here's my advice. Set up (or update) a solid business plan, double check all your investments against the principles I'll be sharing with you in this book, and figure out just how profitable you can expect the business to be.

STILL WITH ME?

If what you've read so far sounds like this book is for you, and if you agree with the stated business objectives, you may decide to keep reading. But I have to warn you about something before we move forward: I'm going to be challenging a lot of preconceived notions about how call centers should work. Specifically, I will be challenging common ideas about the physical layout and structure of the call center and the technology needed to support that structure.

> **TO SUM UP:** In these pages, I'll be challenging you to transform your business. You will need to be willing to invest time, effort, energy, and, yes, some money in this transformation. More important than all of that, you're going to need to change the way you think about selling itself.
>
> If you're willing to make that journey, let's get started.

CHAPTER TWO

Why Traditional Sales Training Doesn't Work

There are lots of different selling systems out there. Unfortunately, most are designed for salespeople who sell face-to-face. These systems are not designed for a three-minute conversation, which, as we've seen, is what happens in a call center.

Your people will need a selling system that has proven effective in the call-center environment, and you will need to train and reinforce that system constantly, if only because the turnover is so high in this industry. So, how can you create a system that works? What do you have to do to set up a sales map that your people can read without difficulty—and actually follow?

THE TRADITIONAL METHODOLOGY

Let's take a look at traditional sales methodologies, which are what most call centers follow. Traditional selling methodologies tend to be focused on a pure numbers game in which little or no rapport is built up with the prospect. The traditional methods typically do not employ what we call "consultative selling"—selling based on intelligent questions that are uniquely relevant to a specific caller. In fact, many people will tell you that because time is at a premium, consultative selling is impossible in a call center.

We reject that theory. We believe that consultative selling can and does work in a call-center environment and that it can deliver results well above the average for your industry—if management is willing to make the necessary investments in time, coaching, design, and technology.

It's true that there is a lot of hype around consultative selling. Many people claim to follow it and train it, but they don't really offer a consultative model. The most respected consultative-selling methodology out there is the Sandler Selling System, which has dominated the world of sales training for the past four decades. The beauty of the Sandler system is its flexibility. It can be adapted successfully to long, complex selling cycles involving multiple decision makers, and it can also be adapted to a transactional sales cycle that plays out in just a few minutes.

The best way to get an understanding of the Sandler Selling System is to look first at what it isn't. In the Buyer-Seller Dance—Sandler's metaphor for a sales interaction—there are always two systems at work: the prospect's system and the salesperson's system. In order to lead in this process, your people must know and apply a selling system that works. They must lead the dance. All too often, however, that's not what happens in a call center. Typically, just the opposite happens—the prospect leads the dance. In the traditional approach, no matter who may seem to be in control of the conversation, the prospect is usually in control of the sales process.

How can you tell? Because it plays out every day. Here is what usually happens when call-center sales representatives engage with prospects.

1. **Prospects don't always tell your people the truth, and they play their cards close to the vest.** It's highly unlikely that your people get good information. Prospects present a less-than-totally accurate picture of their current level of interest, their current situation, and/or their ability or willingness to make a decision on the spot.
2. **Prospects want to know what your people know.** This would be great news if prospects wanted to pay for the information. But they want it for free. Sandler calls this "unpaid consulting." Prospects pick your salespeople's

brains and then run off with the information to do with it what they will.

3. **Prospects don't commit.** Even after prospects obtain pricing or other information they want, it's likely there is more misdirection on the way. They says things like, "Let me think about it; it sounds very interesting. I'll give you guys a call back."

4. **Prospects then disappear.** The connection is severed, but your people may not know it right away. Whether or not your sales cycle incorporates an attempt to follow through, the reality is that prospects have now entered the sales equivalent of the witness protection program. Nothing happens.

A BETTER WAY

When the founder of our company, David Sandler, was developing his selling system, he chose the imagery of a submarine for a radically different, and better, selling model. Why? For one thing, he watched a lot of old war movies. Back in World War II when submarines were attacked, to avoid disaster the crew moved through each compartment, closing the hatch of the previous compartment behind them. David Sandler realized this was a powerful metaphor. The Sandler Selling System requires the same procedure. We train clients on how to move through each compartment, or step, of the selling system to arrive "safely" at a successful sale.

Here's what the process looks like.

1. **Establish Bonding & Rapport (stop acting like a salesperson).** Here, you make the prospect comfortable with you so you can begin to establish a relationship. This is the necessary prerequisite of all consultative selling.
2. **Establish an Up-Front Contract.** Set the agenda for the discussion, and make it clear who's doing what ahead of time.
3. **Uncover and probe your prospect's Pain.** People make decisions emotionally but justify them logically. The most intense emotion that people experience is pain.
4. **Get all the money issues (Budget) out on the table.** You must not only address the cost of your goods or services, but also address the cost prospects will face if they do nothing.
5. **Discover how the prospects make their Decision.** Do the prospects make decisions on their own? Do they get help? Can they make their decision now?
6. **Present a solution (Fulfillment) that will solve the prospects' pain.** The best presentation has little to do with the features and benefits, but it has everything to do with showing your prospects how you can get rid of their pain.

7. **Reinforce the sale with a Post-Sell.** Before parting ways, uncover any problems that will torpedo the deal. Do that while you're still on the call.

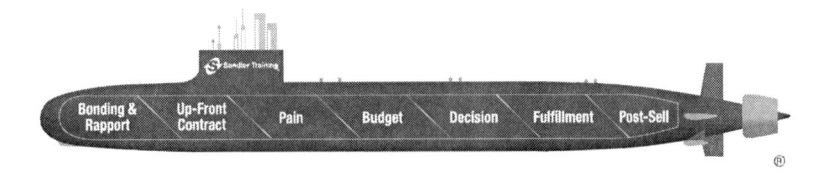

> **TO SUM UP:** The Sandler Submarine is a far more superior sales process than simply following the prospect's system, which is what most call centers use.
>
> Can the submarine work in your call-center environment? The answer is "yes." I'll show you how in the following chapters.

CHAPTER THREE

Communication

You'll recall from our previous chapter that the first compartment of the Sandler Submarine is known as Bonding & Rapport. This is the critical first component. No sale takes place without it, either in a call center or anywhere else. In this chapter, we'll look at some of the elements of effective communication that make bonding and rapport possible. You'll want to understand these basic principles so you can coach and support your team.

THE BASICS

First and foremost, understand that bonding and rapport is not something that you check off a list. It's a constant, ongoing requirement of any good conversation with a prospect (or anyone else). Instead of imagining that a single word or phrase will make someone feel safe and supported during the call, understand that every word of the conversation either improves or degrades the quality of your rapport.

Fortunately, bonding and rapport is relatively easy to establish, and it doesn't take all that much time. Although it's common for outside-selling salespeople to invest an entire meeting building rapport, that's not the way it works in a call center. You don't have that luxury of time. But rapport doesn't need to take three months and countless hours of talking about your hobby or the weather. Rapport can take ten seconds or less, and a good salesperson and sales manager know the moment rapport happens and what to listen for to make sure they have it. (You'll get examples of effective rapport-building a little later on in this book.)

You only have seconds to create an effective bond with a prospect over the phone so it is important that you truly understand the science of rapport.

THE THREE KINDS OF COMMUNICATION

There is a common understanding among the most effective sales professionals that body language, word choice, and tonality all play vital roles in communication with prospects. People communicate in all three of these ways. What follows is good advice for your team, but it's also important for you to bear in mind when it comes to your own communication.

Body Language

Although body language has the biggest impact during a face-to-face meeting, in a call center the tone and body language would trade places. Tonality becomes responsible for most of the communication and messaging sent on the phone.

Please notice, though, that I didn't say body language has no impact on the phone. Body language can definitely affect what comes across on the phone. Haven't you ever talked to someone on the phone and, based solely on the person's tonality, asked, "Why are you so sad?" If you have, you know what I'm talking about. The person you were talking to almost certainly was hunched forward, with shoulders slumped, looking downward. Otherwise, he wouldn't have been sounding sad. Body language definitely does affect the message that comes across on the phone.

Let's try this experiment. Sit up at your desk with your shoulders back, chest out, and back straight sitting upright. Now put a big smile on your face—almost a laugh. Come on, do it. Now think of the saddest thought you can, perhaps when you lost a love one. Can't do it, can you? As I say, body language affects verbal messaging.

Word Choice

People sometimes think scripts make all the difference when it comes to sales effectiveness in a call center. Although sticking to a good script is vitally important, the words you choose only account for a very small portion of the message you communicate over the phone—personally, I'd estimate less than 10%. That doesn't mean words are unimportant. You must create and follow the right script. But you also have to put things in perspective.

Tone

Tone encompasses several items. Let's look at each separately.

Volume

The first key element to tone is volume, or how loud you are, which is a major factor in the ability to establish rapport. On the phone, you want to match your volume to the other person's or perhaps be somewhat less loud than the other person is. The person you are talking with might use volume as a means of controlling the conversation, on the theory that the louder a person is, the more control he has. So if you are coming across as louder than him, that person may feel a loss of control. That's not a great recipe for effective bonding and rapport.

It is certainly OK to increase your volume to make a point or to be clearer, but you don't want to keep your voice at that volume level for long. Teach your salespeople to listen to the volume with the first words uttered by prospects and to respect their volume. There is a time to use volume to take control of the call—you'll learn about that a little bit later in this book—but the increase in volume must occur at the right time.

All too often, call-center representatives come out of the gate at top volume, imagining that this wins them points with the prospect. In fact, this destroys even the possibility of effectively bonding with the prospect.

Make sure your team members know that they should always take their cues on other elements of tone—how high or low they speak, for instance—from the person they are calling.

Pace

This is tougher to measure than volume, but it can be mastered with just a little practice. Get your people to listen to the pace of the other person's voice. If the other voice on the phone is talking slower than you are (and that is often the case), you want to slow down. There are several reasons for this. First and foremost, you want to really listen to this person. Remember, everything he is saying is important to him. That's why he is taking the time to talk.

If the other person is talking faster than you are, that's a sign that he is probably not listening. Instead of talking fast, you might want to slow it down. That helps to slow the other person down.

So, yes, you read right—when in doubt, your people should slow down.

The key to building rapport is not always matching and mirroring. Remember the old commercial when someone was on a train and asked someone else for advice? Everything got silent so the first person could listen. The announcer came on and said,

"When E. F. Hutton speaks—everyone listens." If you want to build rapport and you only have one minute, you need the other person to listen closely, even if it is to your silence. Silence is a critical tool for call-center representatives, but it is too often forgotten.

Timbre

People who work in your call center should learn to ask themselves: "What does my voice sound like? Is it deep or soft, high or edgy? More importantly, can I control it? Can I move from deep to high, from soft tones to harder ones, and back again?"

Have you ever listened to someone and thought, "What a voice!" Have you ever wondered why some newscasters on TV are so effective? It's because of their timbre, the deep richness of their voice, and because of their ability to vary the sounds.

The most effective and successful public speakers understand that the quality of their voice can make the difference between charging $1,000 or $20,000 a session. The very best, highest-paid speakers glide into and out of powerful, deep, soft moments, alternating with effective higher notes, in a way that is almost hypnotic. That's putting vocal timbre to work.

The human voice, well deployed, is an athletic instrument. It requires conditioning, commitment, and continual practice. Here are some exercises you can share for improving the timbre in a team member's voice:

- **Warm up.** Deep breathing and neck rolls are great ways to prepare the voice for the calling day.
- **Breathe from the diaphragm.** All the energy for effective speaking comes from the lower abdomen. Most people breathe from the throat, which can put too much stress on the larynx and reduce vocal power. If your shoulders rise and fall as you breathe, you are not breathing from the diaphragm.
- **Sit up straight.** Better still, make calls from a standing position.
- **Drink plenty of water.** This is a simple step that most call centers ignore entirely. Make sure your team members have access to water, and encourage them to drink lots of it. Coffee actually degrades vocal quality.
- **Don't smoke.** Period.

TO SUM UP: Bonding and rapport is a constant, ongoing requirement of any good conversation with a prospect (or anyone else). How you communicate affects your ability to bond and create rapport with others.

CHAPTER FOUR

More on Bonding & Rapport

I spent a good deal of time in the previous chapter talking about the importance of vocal presentation in establishing Bonding & Rapport—the first compartment of the Sandler Submarine. Obviously, vocal cues have a huge impact on whether your team members create and sustain a good connection with their prospects. This first compartment is so important, however, that it merits a second chapter. Here we'll share other strategies for keeping a solid connection during the call and remind you that, from a call-center standpoint, bonding and rapport really is everything. Again: Rapport must be established almost instantaneously, and it must be sustained throughout the call. If the people you hire can't manage that, you will have problems.

In this chapter, we'll look at some additional strategies and resources for ensuring that there is strong, lasting bonding and rapport during your team's calls with prospects.

BODY LANGUAGE, REVISITED

Let's look more closely at the topic of body language because it's so routinely overlooked in call centers. Some people think body language is not something to manage or control in a call center. As I suggested in the previous chapter, body language is indeed important in this selling environment. Let's take a closer look at body language now.

The best salespeople, whether they realize it or not, use their own body language as a tool for themselves to initiate and sustain their connection with the prospect once the phone conversation begins. Since body language is important to all communication that takes place over the phone, it is important for the call center to promote the use of appropriate body language whenever someone is talking to a prospect. This drives energy and personal presence on the phone.

The first and perhaps most important way to drive good body language is by making sure each of your salespeople has a good headset. Most call centers have good headsets and know the importance of the right equipment. If you were planning on asking your team members to crane their necks to cradle a receiver between their shoulder and ear for hours on end, please reconsider.

That's pretty basic, and most of the companies we work with have no problem equipping their people with good headsets. You can take it a step further, though. You also need to encourage your people to use all the body language they would have been using when having conversations in person. You need to free them up to do exactly what they would do if they were having a conversation in person with the prospect. Yes, that means they should actually stand up once a connection is made with another person, and they need to gesture and use facial expressions that support the emotional content of their message.

This suggestion sometimes comes as a bit of a surprise to our clients. If you're used to thinking of a call center as a place where people are cooped up in little cubicles all day long, a place where people spend most of their calling time seated and hunched over, my challenge here is a pretty simple one: Think again!

A new approach to body language may require you to think outside the box as you become more familiar with the program I'll be outlining for you in the chapters that follow. In fact, this approach may require you to throw the box away. But it is absolutely essential. You will be amazed at the increases in the energy level of your salespeople and the difference this one change makes in moving a prospect through the sales process on the phone.

Unleash your salespeople's natural energy and ability to connect with other human beings. Let them stand up!

Encourage them to stand up the moment they start talking to a prospective buyer. This one simple tactic is an extremely powerful way to transform your team's ability to establish bonding and rapport. This one change will almost certainly result in improved numbers. You can drive the energy up even further if you combine this technique with the open environment floor plan I will describe in a later chapter.

VAK

Sandler uses a communication concept called VAK—visual, auditory, and kinesthetic, the three modalities with which people best interpret information.

VAK is important because most people favor one of these modalities over the others when communicating. For example, a visual person will more likely use visually-oriented descriptive words in a conversation ("see," "watch," "view") and will be more likely to talk at a faster pace than people in the other two modalities. You've heard the expression "a picture is worth a thousand words"? Visually-oriented people are constantly trying to give you the thousand words that match up with the picture in their head. Their visual memories are faster than other people's, and their words always seem to be racing to catch up. They are likely to say things like, "I can see what you mean." Your salespeople should learn to recognize visuals. They should learn to paint a visual picture for these prospects, match their speaking pace, and say things like, "How does that look to you?"

Auditory people will use more sound-oriented verbs, such as "hear," "sound," and "listen." They will probably have a more dynamic tonality to their voice, and, in keeping with that, they typically prefer to talk to someone who speaks in a similarly dynamic tone. Auditory people are likely to say things like, "That sounds good," or "I'm still not hearing you." They are mid-speed talkers. It's important for your salespeople to learn to recognize auditory communicators, too. They should listen carefully to these prospects, match their speaking pace, and say things like, "How does that sound to you?"

A kinesthetic person, also known as a "touchy-feely" type, will use words like "feel," "in touch," or "get a handle on." These folks tend to speak at a much slower pace and use a much softer tone than people in the other two groups. They need you to feel what they are saying. Of course, you want your salespeople to learn to recognize kinesthetic communicators. They should be prepared to slow way down for these prospects, use gentler tone and volume than usual, give them plenty of time to process the message, and say things like, "Does that feel right to you?"

Why is it so important for a good phone salesperson to adjust speed, volume, and word choice to match the other person? Because this will make it easier for the salesperson to establish rapport with people who don't happen to match up with his own modality. Salespeople who only talk on one level will miss out on selling to the other types and will only sell consistently to those with whom they happen to match up.

TAKE THE VAK TEST!

Those who are unfamiliar with the VAK modalities are sometimes a bit skeptical about these processing styles. But it only takes a little experimentation to prove how amazingly accurate the system is. You and your team members can easily identify your own likely modality—visual, auditory, or kinesthetic—by visiting the website teachertools.londongt.org and clicking on Identification and then VAK Questionnaire.

Here's an important point to consider: Assuming you train people properly, the better a job you as manager do of noticing and matching your team members' VAK modalities, the better a job they will do when it comes time to adapt to a prospect on the phone.

TO SUM UP: From a call-center standpoint, bonding and rapport really is everything. The importance of body language in the call-center environment is routinely overlooked. Creating effective body language and noticing and matching VAK (visual, auditory, and kinesthetic) modalities are two important strategies for keeping a solid connection during a call.

CHAPTER FIVE

The Up-Front Contract

An up-front contract is an agreement, made ahead of time, about what will take place during a meeting or discussion—an agreement that clarifies what each person's role in the conversation will be.

This is one of the most powerful and transformative tools Sandler teaches. It's the one best practice I would choose if only one could be adopted by call-center sales representatives. Yet experience has shown that it is the hardest for managers and call-center salespeople to implement. So I'm devoting an entire chapter to it, on the assumption that doing so will make both the underlying theory and the strategic importance of this essential selling tool easier to understand.

To understand why the up-front contract is so essential, why it's worth learning and practicing, you have to remember what we established earlier about the buyer's system and the seller's system. These two systems are totally incompatible, and one or the other is going to be driving the conversation. Someone is going to "lead the dance."

Obviously, when you're operating a call center, you want your people to be the ones leading the dance with your selling system. You don't want them to follow the buyer's process because that generally doesn't turn out well for you. However, the odds seem stacked against your team. How can they possibly assume the initiative on the call given the absurdly compressed timeframe under which they are working, the necessity of building rapport (that's the first compartment of the Sandler Submarine, you'll recall), and the propensity of prospects to shut down whenever they feel they're being sold?

This one simple idea of David Sandler's, the up-front contract, answers that question. It levels the playing field from the very first moments of the call. It not only builds instant rapport with the prospect, but it also gives your salesperson total control over the call—while the prospect thinks just the opposite is taking place.

WINNING HALF THE BATTLE—IN THE FIRST FEW SECONDS

What do people want when they talk to someone who's calling from a call center? They want a feeling of being in control.

The beauty of the up-front contract is that it gives people that feeling—while the call is actually under the full control of the salesperson.

Imagine you're the call-center representative making an outbound call. You make a connection on the other end; someone picks up the phone and says, "Hello." At that moment, the person you're talking to is not in control of the discussion—you are. Now, people don't like not being in control. It makes them uncomfortable. In fact, most people will look for ways to get control back as soon as possible so they can feel comfortable again. The minute people say, "Hello," they're looking for a way to control the call. Without an up-front contract in place, they'll usually try to get that control by saying something like, "Who's calling?" or "What's this in reference to?"

Exactly the same thing happens with an inbound call. Callers call because they have a particular need or a want. They have taken the step of talking to a total stranger about that need or want. It's hard to feel in control in such a situation. These prospects, too, are looking for a way to control the call. Their guard is up, and they are less likely to talk openly. If they feel like they're not keeping control of the call, they're likely to say something like, "I'm just looking," or "I'll call you back later."

What do these two kinds of prospects have in common? The answer is simple. They're uncomfortable.

Your job is to make people comfortable as fast as possible. This can be done quite easily with a well-done up-front contract, one that clarifies exactly what's going to happen during the discussion.

Notice that I said, "a well-done up-front contract"—not one that you think might be better than the one I'm about to describe. A good up-front contract must contain all the ingredients I'm about to share with you, not just the ones you want to put in. The reason I emphasize this is that the one key ingredient that makes the up-front contract truly effective is often an ingredient that people, particularly managers of call centers, tend to want to leave out: giving customers permission to say "no" and leave the discussion whenever they want.

Yes, this actually means that in the early stages of the call, your call-center salespeople are going to tell prospects to go ahead and hang up if they like. You might as well get used to that idea now because it's the only way you can benefit from the rest of what I'll be sharing in this book. Giving prospects permission to hang up is the only way to make absolutely sure they feel comfortable.

Suppose you're the prospect and I'm the call-center representative. My job is to make you as comfortable with talking to me as I can as quickly as possible. Remember, I must establish bonding and rapport within just a few seconds. What better option do I have than saying, "We might not be right for you. If that is the case just let me know, and I'll hang up"?

Now here's the paradox. This kind of statement appears to give you, the prospect, complete control over the phone call. Actually, though, the minute you say, "OK, go ahead" (and that is almost always what happens), you just gave control of the call back to me!

In a call-center environment, the most important words from the prospect are the ones that translate as, "Go ahead. I'll listen." Without that, you have nothing. That's what giving the prospect permission to say "no" does—it makes it much, much more likely that your people will hear that willingness to keep talking.

If one of your salespeople can get someone to say, "Go ahead. I'll listen," and then agree to some simple ground rules for the conversation, half the sales battle is over.

ELEMENTS OF AN EFFECTIVE UP-FRONT CONTRACT

In order for your team members to sell effectively in a call center, they must understand and implement certain non-negotiables. They must incorporate the following elements of an up-front contract before they do anything else on the call. Please consider sharing the following summary with your team members, having them use it without changing anything, and reinforcing it over time.

Creating an Up-Front Contract

1. **Appreciation and Time**

Thank the prospect for his time and say how long you expect this call to take. Remember how irritating it is to think a discussion is going to take five minutes and then realize that it will end up taking far longer? Have you ever gotten one of those emails asking you to do a survey that will "only take a few minutes of your time," and then after about question number 48 abandoned the survey? That's not what you want the prospect to feel. If this is an outbound call, tell the person how much time is needed before the first decision. If this is an inbound call, say how much time you will need to tell him about the offer. Notice that you clarify how long the call will take before you move on to the next steps below.

2. The Agenda

Briefly tell the prospect what is about to take place. Explain the process of the next few minutes. Explain what your role in the conversation will be and what the role of the person you're calling is. Note that when I say "briefly," I mean just a very few words.

3. The Outcomes

There are different possible outcomes. One of those outcomes is that the prospect can tell you "no." Tell the prospect that if he doesn't like what he hears, it is perfectly OK to tell you "no" and you will accept his answer and go away. On the other hand, if there is a reason to keep talking, that's an OK option, too. Ask for affirmation on those being the two possible outcomes of the call. Proceed.

You'll notice that I haven't yet given you or your team a

"script" that reflects a good up-front contract. That's because there are dozens—hundreds—of variations on this basic outline. Don't worry about scripts yet. The key right now is not to focus on a specific script, but to understand the importance of your team incorporating all of the elements I've just shared, including the part where the other person gets to say "no." Having said that, you're probably curious to learn what this sounds like in action. Before we move on to the next chapter, take a look at these examples of what a good up-front contract sounds like—but remember as you read them that the contract your team uses must be customized to your world and must be incredibly concise.

Outbound Up-Front Contract

1. **(Appreciation and Time)** Mike, thank you for picking up the phone. I'm with ABC Energy. Can I take 30 seconds of your time...
2. **(Agenda)** ...and tell you why I called? If there is no interest...
3. **(Outcome)** ...you can go ahead and hang up.

This extremely condensed version gives you a sense of the kind of time scale I'm talking about. What you just read has proved extremely effective in many, many call-center scripts. Here's a longer variation that gives you a sense of the kinds of adaptations you can make.

1. **(Appreciation and Time)** Mike, thank you for picking up the phone. I'm with ABC Energy, and I'm a little uncomfortable making this call. Can I take 30 seconds...
2. **(Agenda)** ...to tell you what this is about? If there is no interest...
3. **(Outcomes)** ...you can tell me to hang up, but if there is a fit, I will get you the information you need.

Inbound Up-Front Contract

1. **(Appreciation and Time)** Mike, thanks for calling the number on the postcard. Can I take 30 seconds...
2. **(Agenda)** ...to tell you what this is about? If you have no further interest...
3. **(Outcomes)** ...you can go ahead and hang up, but if there is some more interest, I can fill you in on the rest of the story.

> **TO SUM UP:** An up-front contract allows your team to win half the battle within the first few seconds of the call. It's an agreement, made ahead of time, about what will take place during a meeting or discussion—an agreement that clarifies what each person's role in the conversation will be. The chapter you just read covers the mandatory elements of the up-front contract; you should know these so you can share them with your team.

CHAPTER SIX

Pain

As we've seen, a well-executed up-front contract does two amazing things simultaneously in the call-center environment. It puts your people in full control of the conversation, and it establishes bonding and rapport with their prospects. As a result, if your people follow the guidelines just shared, they will be in the position to move forward to the third compartment of the Sandler Submarine, Pain.

Before we talk about that, though, a reminder is in order: Bonding and rapport must be sustained throughout the call. That's another way of saying that if the prospect ever doesn't feel safe talking to you, you can expect him to shut down. If he shuts down, you lose. So think of the bonding and rapport stage as an ongoing step, a kind of fuel that supports the forward movement of the entire discussion.

NOW WHAT?

Let's assume that the up-front contract is in place, and it has done its job. Your salesperson has someone on the phone who is comfortable and who has agreed to listen to him for 60 seconds or so.

What does the salesperson do next? Hook the prospect—not by telling the prospect about what your company does, but by asking the right questions.

I realize it may come as a shock to read this, but the hard truth is that people don't care about your product or service. They only care about themselves and their problems or needs. The goal is to get prospects to tell your salespeople that they have a problem or need and for the salespeople to understand what it is so they can fit a solution to match it.

People buy because they have a need or a want, a pain or a pleasure. Until your salespeople uncover that, there is no reason for prospects to buy. Period.

The gap between where people want to be and where they are is called pain. If the call uncovers pain, there's a chance your salesperson can close the sale. If it doesn't, there isn't. It's that simple.

THE INDICATOR LIGHT

I always explain the Sandler concept of pain to people by using an example from my own personal life. I drive a Ford F150 truck with all the bells and whistles. One day, I was out driving and I saw that the screen on my dashboard read, "Right rear tire low." That is what I call a problem. I solved the problem by getting air in my tire that weekend.

About two weeks later, the same message came on again. Again, that was a problem. I solved it by putting air in the tire again.

Then about five days later the message came on again. This time, I put air in the tire, went to the tire store, and asked about buying new tires. The salesman there gave me several options and prices. I said, "I'll think about it."

That Sunday night, I went to the airport and was out of town for three days. When I came back and saw my truck in the parking lot, guess what I had?

When I ask that question during training programs, everyone always says "A flat tire." But actually, that wasn't what I had! What I had was pain.

I immediately called my car dealer and told him I was driving in on a flat tire. Could he put four new tires on the car ASAP?

He said, "Sure, let me get you a price."

I said, "Listen, I don't care all that much about how much it costs. The thing is, I need to get it done now."

My next question for you is: At whom do you think I was mad?

Most people say I was mad at myself, but actually I was mad at the tire salesperson, the one I called after the third instance of the low-tire message. He could have easily said to me, "Sir, I understand you want to think about it, but what happens if you go to work on Monday and you come out, you have a flat tire, and you have to fix it? I can handle it right now to make sure that doesn't happen."

With one simple question he could have prevented all of my pain! You know what? If he'd asked me that, I would have bought the tires.

So here's the big question: How many of your potential customers are mad at you because you didn't ask the right question—the question that would uncover the pain and make the person take action?

I could write a whole book about uncovering pain with effective questions (and I suspect a couple of people already have). For now, I don't want you to get distracted with trying to identify the precise "right questions" for your call center. When we get to the scripting chapter, we will talk about developing the right questions. All I want you and your people to do right now is remember what David Sandler, the founder of Sandler Training, famously said about the sales process:

"Selling is what takes place when you lead the prospect through a step-by-step process, each step of which may lead to the prospect's disqualification and removal from the process. If you do not disqualify the prospect opportunity, the sale moves forward, and eventually culminates in the prospect making a buying decision."

The upshot here is that, assuming the salesperson does the job properly, qualifying or disqualifying a prospect are each equally valuable activities. That's an important point for you, the manager, to understand. If you don't understand it, there's no way your people are going to understand. If the salesperson uncovers pain, the prospect has passed the first threshold for being qualified and the sales process can move forward. If the salesperson doesn't uncover pain, the process can't move forward.

THE BIGGEST QUESTION OF ALL

In a call-center environment, the step-by-step process Sandler was talking about must focus on one incredibly important question. It's a question that you must answer within a very narrow time window: Is there sufficient pain for the person you're calling to take action to remove that pain?

Typically, if you're a salesperson in a call center, you're going to figure that out very quickly by asking just one or two carefully chosen questions. If there is pain, you will move forward to the next compartment of the submarine. If there isn't, the prospect is disqualified, and you move on to someone else.

This Pain Step deserves close consideration, so we'll be looking at it in depth next. You'll get a clearer sense of what good pain questions sound like in the following chapter.

(Note: The call-center sales cycle is so compressed that it makes sense to look at the Pain and Budget Steps of the Sandler Selling System at the same time, which is what we'll be doing next.)

> **TO SUM UP:** The selling process focuses on one incredibly important question: Is there sufficient pain for the person you're calling to take action to remove that pain?

CHAPTER SEVEN

Budget

Most people who work in call centers hear the words "Budget Step" and imagine that this part of the process is going to be a lot more difficult than it is. In fact, if you've got a good script that focuses on pain questions that are relevant to the typical prospect, Budget is quite a simple step that almost takes care of itself. Once you identify the pain, all you are really doing is confirming the prospect's willingness to take action by spending the time, the attention, and, yes, the money necessary to solve the problem.

It is very easy to handle the Budget Step if you follow the Sandler Selling System. Of course, the Pain Step comes first.

Here's how it might work. A salesperson, Bruce, has contacted a prospect, Maria, and he's reached the Pain Step. He's now talking to Maria about the machinery in her plant going down. He asks Maria, "When the machine goes down for a day, what does that cost you?"

(That's what a good pain question sounds like, by the way.)

Maria says, "It costs us $250,000 a day. And it's gone down four times this year."

Of course, that's a million dollars. So what happens next? Ideally, Bruce says, "So it looks to me like you have a million-dollar problem. What would you spend to fix that?"

(Another great question!)

It's very easy to discuss budget once you have established bonding and rapport, agreed upon an up-front contract, uncovered the pain, and used good questioning to monetize that pain. That process gives you the numbers with which to work.

By the way, notice how different the discussion I just shared with you is from what most salespeople do. Most salespeople hear Maria say, "I have a problem—our machine goes down," and then respond with, "OK, what's your budget to fix the machine?" Naturally, Maria is going to say something along the lines of, "As cheap as I can get." That's not the best way to handle the Budget Compartment.

CLOSING THE BUDGET COMPARTMENT IN A SINGLE DISCUSSION

In a face-to-face meeting, it might take the salesperson several meetings to work through all the pain and generate all the pain numbers. Remember though, in a call center, everything is condensed. I'll give you an example of how this step works in a call center in just one call. What you're about to read is based on a real experience from one of my clients.

Bill is a call-center representative working for a collection agency. He calls accounting departments to help them with their bad-debt collection. When he talks to prospects, he works his way through the opening of the call—he establishes bonding and rapport and sets an up-front contract—and then asks, "Tell me about your worst debt. How long has that debt been on your books?" (What compartment is he in when he asks that question? You guessed it: Pain.)

Jamal, the accounting manager Bill is speaking to, says, "That's been on our books for nine months."

"OK," Bill says. "And that debt is how big?"

"$110,000."

"So what do you think that $110,000 has cost you over the last nine months?"

"Well, we've certainly lost all the profit on that purchase, I know that much."

"Which would be about how much?"

"$20,000."

"OK. If I collect that debt for you, what would you be willing to pay me to fix that $20,000 problem?"

"Hmm. We'd be willing to pay you $10,000."

"Well, that works for us. That's what we're going to charge you to collect it: $10,000."

Typically, the call-center representative knows the price before the call even starts. Bill is going to know ahead of time whether that's the right amount to charge.

ANOTHER EXAMPLE OF THE CONDENSED BUDGET DISCUSSION

I'll give you another example of how this works in one discussion over the phone. One of my clients is a university that sells alumni directories to graduates. Its call-center people are working from leads, usually postcards or electronic messages from someone requesting information about how to obtain an alumni directory. Here's a hypothetical call from them.

A call-center representative Marco calls the prospect Rina, works through the opening of the discussion, and says, "I'm just curious—why would you inquire about a directory? Typically, when people reach out to us, it's because they've lost touch with one or two friends. Is that true in your case?" (That's a pain question.)

Rina replies, "Well, yes. I've fallen out of touch with two of my best friends from college, Barbara and her sister Karen. I can't find them online. I can't find them anywhere."

"What would it be worth to you," Marco asks, "if you could get in touch with Barbara and Karen today?" (That's a budget question, but notice how closely it is connected to the answer to the pain question Marco just asked.)

Suppose Rina says, "Well, I'm getting married, and it would really mean a lot to me if they were there. I guess it would be worth at least a couple hundred dollars."

Rina's in luck. The directory is only $75. Of course, if she had no close friends she was trying to get in touch with, Marco wouldn't have gotten that far. Instead, he would have identified a *no*, which is fine. No pain—no sale!

Here's the big takeaway about the Budget Step: In a call-center sales environment, the quality of your pain questions immediately determines the quality of the budget questions you pose.

As you've probably gathered, identifying the right pain questions is a big part of scripting, which we'll be talking about later in the book.

TO SUM UP: If you have a good script that focuses on pain questions that are relevant to the typical prospect, the Budget Step almost takes care of itself. Once you identify the pain, all you are really doing is confirming the prospect's willingness to take action by spending the time, attention, and money necessary to solve the problem.

CHAPTER EIGHT

Decision

The next compartment of the Sandler Submarine is called Decision. This is where people on both sides of the discussion—the salesperson and the prospect—get clear about what the decision-making process is going to be. If you've handled the previous compartments correctly, the kind of clarity I'm talking about comes very quickly and very naturally.

This is where the prospect and the salesperson get their heads around the process that will lead either to a clear *yes* or a clear *no*. Either outcome is OK.

Everyone has a decision-making process—not just for making purchases, but for all life choices, big or small. In a sales process, it is important to know who and what are involved with that process. It could be different with every company you approach. In the call-center environment, it's very likely that you already know, in a broad sense, the decision process that your prospects are likely to be using. At this point of the discussion, your salesperson typically wants to confirm those assumptions through good questioning. Whether your people are talking to a husband and wife about a garage-door opener or to a CFO about a transition to a new piece of software, they need to have an understanding, ahead of time, about how people will be making the decision, and they have to use that knowledge to your advantage.

HOW AND WHY PEOPLE MAKE BUYING DECISIONS

A few words are in order here, just by way of background, about what actually goes into a decision to buy something. David Sandler famously noted, "People make buying decisions emotionally and then justify those decisions intellectually." Let's take a close look at what he meant. This graphic will help.

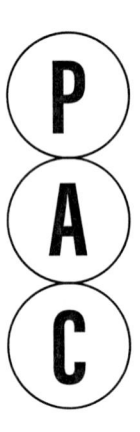

P
A
C

There are three dominant scripts—you can think of them as ego states or voices—which adults carry around all the time. They are the Parent, the Adult, and the Child.

The Parent ego state is where information about good/bad, right/wrong, appropriate/inappropriate is stored.

The Adult ego state is the logical, analytical, rational part of a person's brain that weighs pros and cons, pluses and minuses, upsides and downsides. Think Mr. Spock from the original Star Trek series. "That's logical," or "That's not logical."

The Child ego state is all about emotions and feelings, wants and desires. It's the voice that says, "I want this," or "I want that." It also says, "I don't want this," or "I don't want that."

As sellers seeking clarity about the decision-making process, your people need to understand that not only do they have this scripting constantly at play, the prospective buyers with whom they interact do, too. Buyers behave in certain broadly predictable ways. When David Sandler said that buyers make decisions emotionally and justify them intellectually, he meant that these decisions are typically initiated by something the Child wants or doesn't want—some emotional gap between where the person is now and where he wants to be. As you know by now, we call this gap pain.

I mention all this because the Decision Step, like the two steps before it, assumes the existence of some kind of pain that you can resolve for the prospect. It's vitally important that you understand what drives or doesn't drive a decision to purchase because you are operating in hyperspeed in the call-center environment. It's likely that the Pain, Budget, and Decision Steps will sometimes seem to run together in quick succession. In fact, though, they are three distinct steps.

The existence of pain, in and of itself, isn't a final decision. However, the way the Parent and Adult ego states respond to that pain does generate a decision of some kind. There's either going to be a choice to take action to remove the pain or a choice not to. It all depends on how strong the pain is and how the Parent and Adult ego states frame the internal discussion about the prospect's experience of the pain.

In a call-center environment, a good question sequence that illuminates the pain is one that tends to uncover what your people need to know about budget and decision—in very short order.

EXAMPLE: THE COLLECTION AGENCY

A good example of how the discussion about pain initiates the discussion about budget and decision can be found in the true story of a collection agency with which I worked. (I mentioned this company in the previous chapter.) In this particular call center, there were over 40 salespeople on the phones, calling only CFOs about the prospect company's bad—and seemingly uncollectable—debt.

We had to be clear about what the decision process was going to be when speaking to these executives. In general, CFOs could make the decision immediately as to whether or not to turn a bad-debt account over to us. We'd talked to lots of CFOs in the past about this kind of thing so we had the benefit of experience. Of course, that didn't guarantee we knew what an individual CFO's decision process was going to be. All that meant was we could position ourselves to ask intelligent questions that clarified the individual's decision process.

Occasionally when we raised the issue on the call, CFOs might say they needed to consult with their comptroller to discuss which debt they would turn over to us. Whenever this happened, we would ask them the name and size of the account they were most likely to discuss with their comptroller. In almost every case, the CFO would freely tell us the name and value of the account. Then we would ask what the comptroller might say when asked whether or not his company was doing a good job of collecting on that debt. This question usually provoked a thoughtful pause in the conversation.

We'd continue by asking, "What would it sound like if your boss called you and asked you if you needed help doing your job? What would you say?"

I can't tell you how many times this simple question sequence threw the spotlight on the prospect's pain (the uncollected dollars the CFO knew lay within that account), and then led to an in-depth discussion of budget and decision. Many times a well-placed question like this would get the CFO to say, "You're right. I have this one account [pain] that has been bugging me. What can you do?" At that point, the CFO typically started talking about budget (what it would cost to work with us) and the decision-making process (what would have to happen in order for us to call the account and try to collect).

A word of warning: Your salespeople should know that the decision-making process is not always as complicated as the person they're talking to might initially make it sound. Sometimes it is, of course, but usually it just takes a few good questions to figure out how someone is going to decide whether or not to work with you.

> **TO SUM UP:** The Decision Step is where people on both sides of the discussion—the salesperson and the prospect—get clear about what the decision-making process is going to be going forward.

CHAPTER NINE

Fulfillment and Post-Sell

In the call-center environment, which as we have seen moves quite quickly, I sometimes consolidate the last two steps of the Sandler Submarine into a single stage of the sale, the Presentation Stage. Yet two very different things are happening here. Although they tend to happen quite quickly, they must be understood as separate steps.

The Fulfillment Step is the first step in the closing phase of the Sandler Selling System. It is the result of successfully completing the Pain, Budget, and Decision Steps, and obtaining the prospect's commitment to consider your presentation and make a decision. If your product or service can remedy the prospect's pain for an investment that is within the budget and presented in a manner consistent with the decision-making process, it makes sense to discuss how your product fulfills the specific needs and requirements you've discussed with this person.

David Sandler had a great rule: "The best presentation [is the one] the client never sees." Nowhere is this more accurate than in a call center. The best presentation is minimal, and the very best presentation can hardly be noticed at all.

For example, assume a CFO talking to a sales representative of a collection company asks, "How would you collect a bad debt if I gave you one?"

Here's how the dialogue might unfold:

Salesperson: I would love to run you through that process. Do you have a particular bad debt in mind?"

CFO: Yes.

Salesperson: Might I inquire how much it is for?

CFO: $100,000.

Salesperson: And how old is it?

CFO: 200 days.

Salesperson: I'm curious. How much do you feel you have lost already in 200 days?

CFO: Maybe 30%.

Salesperson: So let me ask you something. If I run through our three-step process and you don't like it, hang up on me. But if you do like it, can I get started today?

Here's a similarly accelerated presentation that typically takes place within the university directory sale.

Prospect: Does it have contact information for everyone with whom I went to school?

Salesperson: It has as close to 100% as we can get. Do you have an old friend in mind that you would like to contact?

Prospect: Yes.

Salesperson: How long has it been since you talked to this person?

Prospect: Oh, at least 25 years.

Salesperson: Would you like to know the email as well?

Prospect: That would be great.

Salesperson: Our directories have name, address, email address, and about 80% of the phone numbers.

And so on. Now, let's assume that the verbal presentation your call-center representative delivers goes well. What's next? The Post-Sell Step serves to "lock up" the sale and facilitates the transition to product or service delivery.

Why do we have such a step? It's not unusual for prospects to have second thoughts after making a positive buying decision. They're likely to wonder whether they made the right decision, whether they paid too much, whether they should have checked with someone before buying, whether your company will really deliver as promised—any number of questions. Unless those unasked questions are addressed, the prospect may be tempted to back out of the decision. So the first order of business in the Post-Sell Step is to bring up those unanswered questions. This allows prospects to express any lingering doubts that might cause the sale to unravel. Sometimes salespeople are tempted to skip the Post-Sell Step—maybe because they imagine a prospect's doubts or questions will go away if only they avoid talking about them. That's a fantasy. In the real world, you want to deal with those doubts and questions while you are still on the phone with the prospect.

Here's how the post-sell might sound with that CFO:

Salesperson: We are going to get started on collecting this debt today. After 10 days I will call you back and let you know where we stand. If I collected your debt, can we talk about doing more business together?

Here's how it might sound in that university directory discussion:

Salesperson: Now that you are all set to get your directory, maybe you can help me. You probably are still in contact with some college buddies who might want one of these. Would you be comfortable giving me their emails or phone numbers so I can get them one of these as well?

The post-sell is also an opportunity to discuss future business and request referrals, if that's appropriate to your call center's sale.

REMEMBER: THE PRESENTATION COMES LAST

The Presentation Stage is usually something we script out carefully, but no script can succeed if we have not made our way through the previous compartments of the Sandler Submarine. This part of the process doesn't occur until all the other steps have been completed. It's tempting to rush forward to presentation because this is the part where you tell prospects all the wonderful things your products or services can do. But you must never, ever deliver the presentation prematurely.

It's natural for your salespeople to want to talk about the things they think will make people want to buy your products or services. The presentation will be much simpler and far more effective, though, if the salespeople take their time and confirm that they have done all the previous steps correctly.

By the way, If you want to learn more about the Sandler Selling System, I recommend the book *You Can't Teach a Kid to Ride a Bike at a Seminar* by David Sandler. It gets into a lot more depth on the system itself. I've limited myself to giving you a basic overview here, but it's an overview that is detailed enough for anyone on your call-center team to be able to execute what follows.

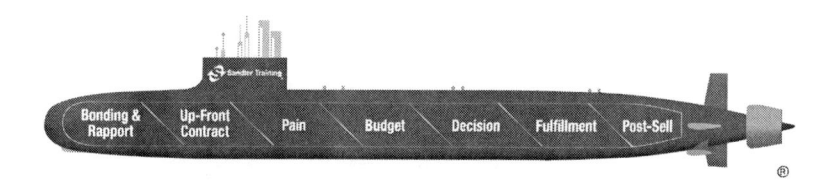

Later on in the book, we will be putting this all together so you can see how everything flows. Before we do that, though, it's time to look more closely at the physical layout of your call center.

> **TO SUM UP:** The Fulfillment Step is the first step in the closing phase of the Sandler Selling System. It is the result of successfully completing the Pain, Budget, and Decision Steps, and obtaining the prospect's commitment to view your presentation and make a decision. The Post-Sell Step serves to "lock up" the sale and facilitates the transition to product or service delivery.

THE ENVIRONMENT AND THE PEOPLE

CHAPTER TEN

BAT and the Call-Center Environment

The purpose of this important chapter is to give you control over the single most powerful positive force for maximizing a call-center team's potential: the physical environment in which they work.

As you might imagine, I've spoken to a great many managers and executives about call-center sales teams over the years. Most of them are surprised to hear me insist that changing the physical environment is the most important step they can take when it comes to enhancing sales performance—more important than recruiting the right people, more important than your compensation plan, even more important than creating the right script for people to use.

Perhaps you're surprised at all this, too—and perhaps you're a little skeptical. Perhaps you were expecting, when you got to the heart of this book, to find a discussion of the techniques necessary to ensure success. If that's the case, please keep reading.

THE SUCCESS TRIANGLE

The Sandler Selling System holds that success depends not just on specific procedures—on technique—but on two other elements: behavior and attitude.

These three elements of success—behavior, attitude, and technique—are known as the Success Triangle, and the three have to be balanced to make everything work.

Confidence
Outlook
Responsibility

ATTITUDE

SUCCESS

TECHNIQUE

BEHAVIOR

Goals
Plans
Actions

Strategy
Preparation
Focus

Behavior is "muscle memory," something you've trained yourself to do automatically. Attitude is your internal self-talk about who you are and what you're doing. Technique is the specific procedure you're responsible for implementing.

Most of the executives and owners I talk to want to focus exclusively on technique when we talk about their team. They miss a critical point: If any one point of the Success Triangle is underdeveloped, performance collapses. Your people can have great technique, but if no one is accountable for using it on hourly calls (behavior), the technique will never mature to success. (Some call-center managers experience this and conclude, wrongly, that technique doesn't matter in a call-center environment.) You can have a great attitude, but if there's no mastery of technique and no daily routine of behavior, the results will be lackluster. (I'm sure you can think of a couple call-center representatives who fall into that category.) Likewise, have you ever worked with someone whose attitude was so negative that it undercut any positive achievements in the area of technique or behavior? (I have.)

The bottom line here is that just telling people what to do is not enough. In fact, it's not even close to enough.

You must remember that any time you or one of your fellow human beings try to adopt and implement a new technique, you will feel uncomfortable. That's just a fact of life. Largely because of that discomfort, you will probably do it poorly at first. You will probably fail. So you may want to revert back to your old way of doing things, not because it is better but because it is easier. That goes for you, for me, and for everyone on your selling team. It's just how human beings are wired.

In order for your call-center team members to implement the good ideas—the techniques—you'll be sharing with them, they will have to become comfortable with the possibility of going outside of their comfort zone over and over again. That's a big deal, and the physical environment in which they work is going to have a major impact on whether or not they actually do it for you.

Most of the executives and owners I speak to don't believe me when I say all this about the difficulty of expanding one's comfort zone. They just want me to "train the team" and leave the physical layout of the call center alone. They assure me that their team will eventually pick up whatever techniques I share during the training. I ask them to consider taking part in the following experiment.

YOUR MORNING ROUTINE

Try this experiment tomorrow morning when you get up. Brush your teeth using your non-dominant hand to hold the toothbrush. For example, if you typically brush your teeth with your right hand, use your left.

At this point, I have a prediction to make. The first thing that will happen tomorrow morning is that you will forget about the experiment until you are finished brushing your teeth. In fact, this might happen for a couple of days in a row—until you put a sticky note on your mirror to remind you. When you finally remember to do the experiment, you will find one of two things: It will take you way longer than it usually does to brush your teeth, or you will do such a bad job that you will instantly want to revert back to the usual way of brushing.

Don't.

Leave the sticky note up to remind you. Keep brushing with your non-dominant hand until you get good at it. Once that is done, try going back to the old way. It will seem hard.

The point of the exercise is to illustrate to you that whenever people expect to change a behavior, they must have constant reminders (like that sticky note) to make sure they actually do change.

Please commit to conducting this experiment, not just reading about it. You may cheat once in a while because you don't have time, but you must also be aware of what's happening, and you must be prepared to be uncomfortable. There's a point to all this: When you ask for changes, your people will be uncomfortable, too. At Sandler, this discomfort is called pushback.

> *"Resistance to change comes in code: i.e., 'This doesn't apply to our industry.'"*
> —Tom Krasten, CEO of Levi Strauss

CLOSE-UP ON ATTITUDE

Now that you've got a clear sense of what a major undertaking it is to change a behavior, let's talk in a little more depth about attitude.

The call center must create an environment where the attitude is consistently high. Please notice that I did not say positive. This is because David Sandler used to say, "I don't believe in positive mental attitude. You should be depressed if you can't make your mortgage payment."

The right attitude doesn't have to be positive. A strong attitude, positive or negative, can be productive if you can create a feeling of success and harness that strong attitude.

Too often I find people in call centers trying to create a positive attitude and failing, instead of harnessing the strong different attitudes already in the room to create a sense of purpose—a sense of "getting it done." That's what I mean by creating an environment where there's a consistently high attitude. The physical structure of the work environment has a huge role to play in that.

This is where most managers come up short. They think smiling a lot, putting up posters, praising people, and repeating phrases like "Think Positive!" will change the team's attitude. Unfortunately, they're wrong. Attempting to mandate a cheerful, positive attitude in the call center never works. All it does is alienate the team and make the attitude problem even worse.

If you're interested in improving the attitude in the room, accept people as they are and where they are. Focus on big, achievable goals that inspire people and improve the team's overall cohesion—that indefinable sense of belonging to a group that is pointed in the right direction. This group dynamic is, potentially at least, an extremely powerful force, particularly in the closed environment of the call center. Why? Because people are likely to change the way they think of themselves when they act as part of a group. Performance is always consistent with the way people view themselves conceptually. If you're like a lot of the people I work with, you're still wondering, "OK, but what does all this talk about behavior, attitude, and technique have to do with the environment of a call center? Why do I need to change the layout if I want to support the Success Triangle?"

Experience has shown that the right call-center environment can and does harness that purposeful, high-performance attitude we've been discussing. It also improves the daily behaviors and makes it easier for people to adopt and master successful new techniques.

Experience has also shown that the wrong call-center environment can do just the opposite.

The right work environment is the single biggest factor in the success or failure of a call center. It should be—but only rarely is—consciously designed. For your call center, that changes now.

CONSIDER THE PSYCHOLOGY

Most call centers have anywhere from 10 to 100 people sitting in cubicles in a single shared workspace, either answering or dialing the phone. What are the psychological demands of the job that must be performed in such a space? Remember, you want your person to talk to 100–200 people each day.

Let's begin, not with the call-center representative, but the person to whom you're trying to sell. Think of the person picking up the phone on the other end. You are interrupting that person's day. That's the essential first dynamic of that conversation. That's what you have to understand going in.

In the inbound-call scenario, think of the person who might be calling the call center from an ad. What does that person want? Most likely, he wants information and then wants to hang up.

What's the common element you have to be aware of in either situation? No one wants to be sold! In fact, when you try to sell them stuff, what happens? People yell at you, don't want to talk to you, and sometimes even call you names.

At this point, I have to ask you about the people working in your call center. Stop and think about this for a moment. You offered each and every one of them a job. They accepted. Can we agree that the reason someone wants a job where people yell at them, don't want to talk to them, and call them names is money?

If it isn't money, I don't know what it is. They certainly didn't accept your job offer because they were convinced the day-to-day duties of the job would make them feel good about themselves or get their emotional needs met. Let's put it this way: If your people are showing up at work each day for reasons other than making money, they may have some other issues that need addressing.

Because the most reasonable motivation for this job is to make money, you must give every appropriate push to make sure your people take every opportunity to make money. In short, you have to give them a cookbook.

Let me explain what I mean by that. Sandler offers salespeople a tool called the Sandler Cookbook for Success. This is created to help team members stay on track and meet their goals.

Why do we call it a cookbook? If you were to open a good cookbook to just about any page, you would find a picture on the top of the page of the outcome you wanted to create, and then, below that, you would find a list of the ingredients, followed by a set of instructions telling you exactly what steps you had to follow in order to cook the dish properly. You might also find notes on temperature, serving size, presentation, and so on. If you follow the instructions, you should get a replica of the picture on top of the page.

If you had an outside-selling salesperson knocking on doors, the Cookbook for Success might look like the following illustration.

ACTIVITY	FREQUENCY	MONTH 1		MONTH 2	
		Target	Actual	Target	Actual
Dial	No/week				
Follow-Ups	No/week				
Networking Meetings	No/month				
Networking One-to-Ones	No/month				
Give Referrals	No/week				
Ask for Referrals	No/week				
Touch Base with Past Clients	No/week				
RECONs	No/month				
Client Touches	No/month				
1st Meetings	No/month				
Prospect Meetings (Not 1st)	No/month				
Free Talk Attempts	No/month				
Free Talk Given	No/month				
Social Media Activities	Mins/day				
Mail Shot					
Newsletter					
		Pay time		No-Pay time	

This helps the salesperson track how many calls he made that week, how many appointments he went on that week, how many emails he sent out, how many networking events he attended, and so on. An outside-selling salesperson can look at the cookbook during the week and make sure he is on track and staying on track. This helps a salesperson with behaviors, or how he implements the right techniques on a daily basis. Certainly if he does hit his numbers at the end of the week, attitude can improve. Why? He feels like he is doing all the right things to hit every one of his goals. And he is!

Maybe you're wondering: Are call-center representatives supposed to have a cookbook? The answer is "yes"—but it doesn't look like what you're probably expecting.

THE ENVIRONMENT IS THE COOKBOOK

In a call center, things happen to the representatives at a much faster rate, with far fewer options for making decisions than an outside-selling salesperson has. It's important then to change the nature of the cookbook this person uses accordingly. Use the environment itself to create a special type of cookbook.

After having given the representatives an understanding and a process to make money, you now need to use the other big human motivators—competition and fun. They will come to work for you if they can make money—but it can also be a fun competition. This is why the environment is so important. Your first comment might be, "Well, we can't have all the background noise." The only one hearing the background noise is you, and the benefit the new environment will give you far outweighs the noise. With today's technology, most of the background noise will be subdued.

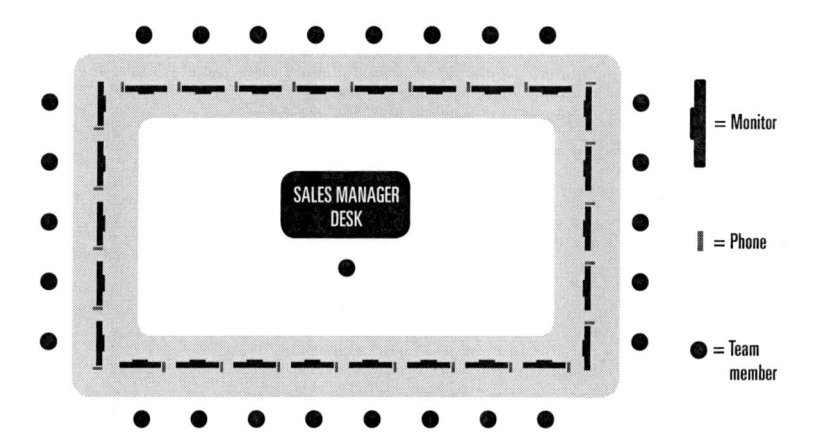

(diagram: rectangular call-center layout with SALES MANAGER DESK in the center, surrounded by team member positions; legend: | = Monitor, ▮ = Phone, ● = Team member)

It's time to get rid of those cubicles and instead create an open environment. We suggest using a large oblong or even round table that holds 20–30 people and their workstations—with the sales manager sitting inside the circle.

Notice how different this layout is and what kind of implications it has on team cohesion. In a cubicle, I can talk to someone on the phone, hang up, and then pause for a moment, make some notes, take a look at some paperwork I have on my desk, have a sip of coffee, look at the clock, and then find the next person I want to dial. In other words: call avoidance heaven.

When I have my own cubicle, I can look at the next name on the list, wonder what kind of person will answer, and take my sweet time before I start dialing the phone. I can even pull up YouTube on my phone and take a look at the highlights from the ball game last night.

On average, these kinds of self-imposed distractions result in five empty minutes (or sometimes even more) between calls. That's wasted time. In a call center, that is expensive. Yet as a person working in a call center who wants to make money, I might not even realize that I'm wasting time. In fact, the odds are very good indeed that, at the end of the day, I don't even know that I just threw away two hours' worth of money-making opportunities.

Now look how different it is when my manager changes the environment. In an open table environment, I hang up the phone and all around me are people on the phone talking to people. Imagine the energy! What do you think the likelihood is of me spending five minutes looking around before I pick up the phone and start dialing? (Or, if we're all using autodialers, what is the likelihood that I'm going to find reasons to take long breaks between calling sessions, if no one else is doing that?) My environment is forcing me to get back on the phone. We typically see a rise in call volume anywhere from 20% to 30% when the cubicles are removed.

THE BIGGEST MISTAKE IN MANAGING A CALL CENTER

I am often asked to identify the single biggest mistake call-center managers make. The answer is easy, and by this point in the book I am hoping you know what it is. The single biggest mistake call-center managers make is putting the call-center salespeople in cubicles or offices.

That's the standard approach, and it's a big problem. Most of the time there is some kind of physical separation between salespeople. That's not what you want. Think about it: If I'm in a cubicle by myself, I can't see anybody else unless I turn my chair around. That means I'm going to be operating from a position of very low energy, and I'm going to stay in that low-energy mode as the day goes forward. I'm working inside my own little world, setting my own pace, and that means I can be driven down very easily.

A successful call center, on the other hand, has a very open environment, where everyone can see everyone else and all the salespeople see and feel the energy of the group.

A lot of managers ask me, "Is it really worthwhile to change the floor plan?" The answer is "yes"—absolutely. Why? Because once you change the floor plan, you will see the number of dials go up, the number of conversations go up, the average talk time go up, the total call volume go up, and the closing ratio go up. All of that happens once you change to an open, high-energy environment. We measure all the key metrics when we do this, and they always go up. It's because of the energy that goes around the room once the walls come down.

One company I worked with had 40 salespeople working in the call center. The very first thing we did was to knock down the walls. No more cubicles, no more walls. Every time you started a conversation with a prospect, you held that conversation around a single huge table that you shared with every other call-center representative. We had forty people sitting around this massive table, making calls. Noise wasn't a problem because the company had invested in noise-cancellation technology.

The rule we set up for the salespeople sitting around that table was very simple. Once you made a connection with someone on the phone and you were actually engaged in a conversation, you had to stand up. You had to conduct the whole sales call on your feet. That raised the energy in the room.

Now imagine: If I'm all alone in my cubicle—if I'm safe behind my three little walls—and I make a call, once that call is done, what do I do? I take a little break, think about how the last call went, and maybe I have a cup of coffee. I probably take a few minutes to wonder whether it's really a good day to sell. After all, that last person I talked to hung up on me.

On the other hand, if I'm in a communal, open environment, and I see all my colleagues on the phone, making calls, trying to make their next connection with a prospect, the dynamic is totally different. I'm going to get right back on the phone when my call is over. If I look around and I see 10 or 20 of those 40 people standing up, and I haven't stood up in 10 minutes, what's going to be going through my head? "I really need to make some dials—everybody else is standing up!" That's the energy in the room—and the power of peer pressure. (By the way, I am emphasizing these points for a reason: Most managers of call centers ignore them.)

Call volume went up 25% in that department when we took down the walls and set up the big table.

INBOUND AND OUTBOUND

Many call-center managers we work with have people answering the phone for inbound calls, but they also want their people to make outbound calls if the phone is not ringing. Guess what happens if I'm sitting in a cubicle compared to an open table?

I make fewer outbound calls. That problem vanishes when you move to an open table environment.

This one change alone can increase sales dramatically—and has!

SUPERCHARGING THE SUCCESS TRIANGLE

So let's examine what this simple work environment change does to our Success Triangle. First, let's look at behavior. How does the physical environment affect people's likelihood to do the behaviors that support them? Well, consider, by way of comparison, a health-club environment. It is open, and you can see everyone else's activity. I'm not sure if you have a health-club membership or will get a chance to go to one and just observe. The next time you're in a health club, you will see this concept alive and well.

Try this. If several people are walking on the line of treadmills and someone gets on in the middle and starts running, watch the speed of the walkers. They may not get to running mode, but they will speed up. I know I do it, each and every time. You will see this same concept alive in the weight-lifting room. It is one of the main reasons people don't lift by themselves. They work with partners, and the partner's activity pushes them.

Now think of your people on a treadmill (the phone) sitting in a cubicle going at any pace they want, as opposed to the treadmill (the phone) in the middle of the room with 40 other people.

Activity drives activity.

You can imagine that in an open environment it is hard to hide and also hard to take breaks. You as the manager don't have to be a slave driver demanding an abundance of calls. It will happen automatically due to the environment. Remember how the Success Triangle works. The increased behavior doesn't make a difference if there is a bad attitude so you need to make sure behavior doesn't affect attitude or technique.

There are always going to be those who are not motivated by others. Their productivity will remain the same no matter what environment they're in. But now it is easy to distinguish the movers from the mediocre players. This will allow you to make an informed decision about them.

Next, let's look at attitude. What kind of attitude do you think gets inspired when there are a lot of people standing around, making lots of noise, or, better yet, making lots of money? In a call center, the sound of money is people talking on the phone. People sitting and working in a call center know they make money when they are talking to people. What kind of attitude do you think you might have if you made 45 calls sitting in a cubicle compared to ending the day with the excitement created by you and your fellow teammates when you end the day with 75 conversations?

In a call center, attitude is most important, but attitude is created by the right behavior. This is proven by those who exercise frequently. How many times have you wanted to forego your daily exercise routine? That's bad attitude. Did you go ahead and exercise anyway? How did you feel afterwards? You created better attitude. Each positive phone call drives attitude through the team.

Of course, it's the same in outside selling. When outside-selling salespeople walk back in the office from a closing appointment, you never have to ask them whether or not they got the order. If they got it, you know the minute they walk in the office. They tell everyone.

Now consider the open environment. What do you think will happen when salespeople hang up the phone after getting an order? They will let everyone know, which will drive up excitement and more. This is activity.

Finally, we come to technique. If people have great behavior and great attitude but bad technique, the first two will quickly dwindle. So how does this new environment help with technique?

Listening to others and their techniques will only help to improve others. Think about sitting alone in a cubicle. What can you learn from yourself if you are sitting in a cubicle? What can you learn from sitting around 20 other people hitting the phones every minute? Your technique must improve.

Again, consider the health-club analogy. When I'm lifting weights with others, they will give me tips. I will also watch as they are running on the treadmill and might even imitate them. If I'm sitting in a room with 40 other people and every couple of minutes someone says, "Got one," I will start listening as the other people work. I might even get up and go ask them, "What is your secret?"

In contrast, if I sit in a cubicle, I have nothing to compare myself to and certainly don't compare myself against the rest of the team. At least not right away. I don't compare myself against the team until the end of the week, when it is too late. An open environment encourages the most meaningful kind of learning—on the spot, experiential learning.

THE PHYSICAL ENVIRONMENT SHOULD TRACK PERFORMANCE

I hope by now I have convinced you that the open environment will increase your bottom line. Now let's look at what else you can do with the environment.

We have only skimmed the surface of the room environment. You now need to drive competition and attitude. This creates excitement. So, what are the hourly goals for the department? What are the hourly goals of the individuals? How do you create a competitive atmosphere to drive even better behavior, better attitude, and better technique using the environment to drive team cohesion and activity?

How about putting 50-inch TVs on all four walls so everyone can see the statistics of the team, which are constantly updated?

Or creating a simple dashboard with some simple bar graphs that keep flashing where people stand? A few different leading indicators could be: number of dials, talk time over three minutes, closes, money. You can make this easy and clear to read. Voila! The environment is your cookbook.

For a simple list, show who is at the top and who is at the bottom. Or, you could use colors. Use green to show the leaders who are over the hourly benchmarks. Use yellow for those right at the numbers, and use red for those under the numbers.

The TVs should be very busy, constantly flashing those numbers and changing every five minutes with new stats. This may sound hard to do, but with today's technology and everyone tied into the same software, it is relative easy and certainly worth the time to do it for the bottom line. Your IT experts can take any CRM and hook it up to TVs to constantly show each person's stats.

A PERFORMANCE INCENTIVE YOU MAY NOT HAVE CONSIDERED

Here's a question: What happens to the person on the televised list who is dead last? In most cases, instant motivation.

Nobody who works in a call center wants to be dead last on the list. If someone is OK with being dead last, he won't last long in any call center. Everyone wants to be at the top of the list. Two things drive salespeople: how much can be made and competition. In a call center, these two factors must be at the forefront of each person's day, all day long.

BAT and the Call-Center Environment

Tom	Juan	Jon	Keiko	Bob	Luke	Bill	Debbie	Don
Number of calls: 38	Number of calls: 36	Number of calls: 34	Number of calls: 30	Number of calls: 29	Number of calls: 18	Number of calls: 18	Number of calls: 14	Number of calls: 11
Talk Time: 43 minutes	Talk Time: 38 minutes	Talk Time: 37 minutes	Talk Time: 38 minutes	Talk Time: 39 minutes	Talk Time: 27 minutes	Talk Time: 29 minutes	Talk Time: 20 minutes	Talk Time: 20 minutes
Number of closes: 5	Number of closes: 4	Number of closes: 4	Number of closes: 4	Number of closes: 3	Number of closes: 2	Number of closes: 2	Number of closes: 1	Number of closes: 1
Joe	Fred	Yvonne	LaToya	Will	Brad	Dan	Jessica	
Number of calls: 10	Number of calls: 8	Number of calls: 7	Number of calls: 7	Number of calls: 5	Number of calls: 5	Number of calls: 5	Number of calls: 5	
Talk Time: 13 minutes	Talk Time: 12 minutes	Talk Time: 10 minutes	Talk Time: 9 minutes	Talk Time: 7 minutes	Talk Time: 7 minutes	Talk Time: 9 minutes	Talk Time: 11 minutes	
Number of closes: 1	Number of closes: 1	Number of closes: 0	Number of closes: 0	Number of closes: 0	Number of closes: 0	Number of closes: 0	Number of closes: 0	

Sample call center monitor readout. The numbers are displayed on a big-screen TV and updated continuously.

By the way, those TVs showing the numbers should not only be in the call room, but in the break room and bathrooms. You will find that people will take breaks less often and get back on the floor faster if they go from green (over performer) to yellow (average performer).

WHITEBOARDS

A great finish you can add to the call room is to make all the walls whiteboards. Use the walls to make the room a little livelier. With markers you can put up relevant numbers: who won the most sales yesterday, who is leading the month, and even whose birthday it is. But the one thing that drives energy more than anything is putting up a template that reads as follows:

Before I leave today I will:

_____

_____

_____

_____

Make sure everyone on your team finishes that statement, in writing, on the board. Everyone gets one line before the shift starts. People don't have to put their name on the wall, but they do have to commit to a written personal goal every day.

CONTESTS

Contests can provide daily or even hourly motivation. Contests bring the physical environment to life by creating some excitement in the lives of the salespeople. You can get them excited about making a few more calls or hitting a team or individual goal by offering a payoff as simple as a $5 gift card. Consumer products they can take home today are also big attention-getters. Almost all call centers we work with have many contests going on at once, with prizes like a kid's bike, a 50-inch TV, or an iPad sitting out on display, just waiting for someone to claim them. This works. Try it!

IT ALL ADDS UP

Think about what these additional steps will do to your team's behavior, attitude, and technique.

The TVs on the wall will certainly drive more behaviors by giving your team members a minute-by-minute benchmark of where they are compared to where they should be. The whiteboard walls will show longer-term statistics and will make it clear to the team what behavior to change in order to catch up for the month. Goals that are written down for all create commitment to specific behaviors for the day.

The TVs and the whiteboard create nonstop excitement and attitude that cannot be hidden. Team members either become part of this attitude or they quit—they can't hide.

This kind of work environment shows exactly where team members have to improve in techniques, how quickly they have to learn techniques, and whom they can learn it from the fastest.

Without a doubt, this makeover of your call center can be a game changer and an immediate improvement for your bottom line.

Commit to making these simple, powerful changes—and don't spend a lot of time looking for reasons to avoid them. For instance, don't tell yourself there's going to be a noise problem. That is a common excuse for inaction. Remember: Technology will help you handle this noisy environment so that it is not an issue for the people your team members are talking to on the other end of the line.

Make the commitment! Take action!

> **TO SUM UP:** The Sandler Selling System holds that success depends not just on specific procedures—on technique—but on two other elements: behavior and attitude. The call center must create an environment where the attitude is consistently high.

CHAPTER ELEVEN

Sales Management

There is a vast difference between call-center sales management and outside-selling sales management. To get a handle on that difference, it's important to first understand the four components of the sales manager's job—in a call center or in any setting.

YOUR FOUR JOBS

Here's an interesting—and important—exercise. Take four pieces of paper. On top of each sheet, write one of these four titles: supervisor, trainer, coach, and mentor. Once you are done doing that, draw a picture of those titles doing their job. Go ahead and make it simple. Use stick figures. There's no penalty for lousy art skills.

Once you've done this exercise, and not before, turn the page.

So—what did your drawings look like?

If you are like the rest of us, your figures probably looked something like this:

- Supervisor: Someone standing over others, pointing, telling them what to do.
- Trainer: Someone at a whiteboard or flip chart pointing at some figures written there.
- Coach: Someone talking to others on a bench or trying to motivate others.
- Mentor: Someone having a one-on-one discussion with somebody else, on an equal level with that person.

Well, if you got anything close to those images—and I'm guessing you did—then you already have a good understanding of the four basic jobs of a sales manager. That means you already have an idea of what you must be skilled at in order to be a good manager. Let's walk through how a brand new salesperson might flow through these roles with you.

Supervisor is the role you play with a new hire. You tell new hires exactly what to do and when to do it: where their computer is, how to log in, how they must complete their reports, what scripts they should use, how they should expect their performance to be measured, and so on. Usually, you don't have to worry about being too nice about any of that. New hires are happy that they have a job and happy to have the opportunity to make some money. This is a critical role for any call-center manager. In fact, in the call-center environment, if this role of supervisor is done poorly, then the rest of the roles almost don't matter. (I say "almost" because, if you were to go out of your way to perform badly in those other three roles, they would matter.)

Here's why they almost don't matter: The supervisor's role is the one that creates all the measurements that are needed to be successful at the job. A good supervisor also creates the process one must follow to do the job correctly. It should sound like this: "If you do A, B, and C, D will happen. You need to do A, B, and C this many times each day to work here." Too many companies ask people to come to work, sit them down, and say, "Welcome aboard. Make D happen."

To take this outside of sales for a moment, let's say you had a manufacturing plant and you just hired a new machine operator. Would you shake that person's hand after hiring him, point him toward the machine, and say, "OK, go run it"? I doubt it. You would probably teach the person how to operate the machine safely, explain how to handle maintenance and repairs, talk about what the operator was expected to accomplish each day, walk the person through how to file reports at the end of the day, and so on. Why should sales be any different?

So what's the takeaway from our discussion of the supervisor role? It's pretty simple. Ask yourself whether you truly have a traceable, measureable process in place for your sales department. If not, go to work. If you need help, call us.

The next role of a manager is **trainer.** Here's how that role plays out. The new hire has been with you for three to six months, depending on your business, and knows what he should be doing. Now the trainer side of you comes out and helps teach this person how to do it better, more efficiently, and perhaps a little quicker. While the supervisor role really isn't all that concerned about the other person's thoughts or feelings, the trainer is. This role is all about making people feel good about themselves and their work, and then passing along advice. The trainer says things like, "Great job. Now let's try this."

There are a couple reasons for this change. For one thing, now that people have been working for a while, they might not be as enthusiastic as before. You need to take time to keep motivating them. In other words, the honeymoon is over. They were so happy with the company and the new job in the past, and they now have had time to see your less flattering side, whatever that is. Every company has a less flattering side, and yours is no exception. Perhaps there were orders that didn't go as well as planned, or there are problems with production, or there is not the greatest marketing in the world. Who knows? At some point, there are going to be problems.

There is no such thing as the perfect company. Everyone messes things up sometimes—the sooner you accept this, the better. The trainer still gives employees direction, but also offers pats on the back, makes sure everyone knows they're appreciated, and keeps them motivated.

After the new recruit has been with you a while and knows what to do and the best way to achieve results, it's time to put your **coaching** hat on. This is one of the hardest roles to get right. There are a number of reasons. It's time to stop telling people what to do or how to do it. That means that, as a coach, you must refrain from saying anything along the lines of, "This is what I would have said," or "This is what you should have done." For most managers, that's quite a challenge, at least at first.

A coach's job is to get the proverbial 110% out of the recruit on game day—or, if you're fussy about the math, to help the person achieve maximum potential. You can't do that by telling the person, in a narrow sense, what to do.

Think of it this way. You're an athlete. During the game, the coach doesn't get to go on the field with you and tell you what to do. The coach relies on the belief that you have had enough training and you know the processes.

That's the assumption to make in a call center. If I have been working for you for six months, why would you have any need to tell me how to do my job? Wouldn't people who have been working for you for the last nine months be more likely to ask you what you would have done? At that point, there is simply no advantage in telling them how you would have done it. The coach's job, instead, is to form good questions: "How could you have handled that differently?"

The thing that gets in the way of becoming a good coach is the big enemy of most sales managers: ego. The sales manager's ego (mine included, by the way, when I was a sales manager) thinks the coaching role is a waste of precious time. The ego wants to tell someone, anyone, "how I would have done it." The ego believes this creates value for its position, but in fact, it does just the opposite. The salesperson says, "OK, I will try that," but never does. The ego says, "Well, at least he's trying." And nothing changes.

A real coach responds with something like this: "You have been here long enough to know three different ways to handle that situation. Before you leave today, come up with three different solutions to tell me about." This way you put the growth and the learning on the other person's shoulders and not on yours. That's a coach!

Most sales managers I talk to tell me they coach their people all the time. Then I share with them what I've just shared with you, and they tell me that what they have really been doing is training. Sit in on a Sandler sales management workshop, and you'll really see the difference.

Now that the employee has been with you a while, you might want to change your role to that of **mentor**. A mentor is someone who will give the right advice—even when not asked.

A mentor is that person who makes the one statement or asks that one question that makes the employee think differently.

Here's the key point. You only become a mentor to those people who have transitioned out of the coaching model. They are doing everything right and hitting their numbers, and they just need a little kick in the rear or a pat on the back once in a while.

Is it possible that someone who has hit the stage of needing a mentor will ever need a supervisor again? Yes. It could be that you have a new product that needs to be introduced and you have to set up the processes and metrics to do this. Perhaps the salesperson could have gone into a slump or lost a big account and needs someone to hold him accountable for getting back to normal.

A lot of sales managers have a hard time with this kind of transition. Someone has been so good for so long that you assume he doesn't need much in the way of help from you. Then he goes into a slump, and you wait for him to "snap out of it."

Waiting is not enough. If you do nothing to help your people, you're not doing your job. You are doing a disservice to your top salespeople by not having the tough conversations they need. They need to be told they are in a slump. Until they get out of the slump, you are taking them back to the basics. You will go back to tracking all their activities and having them report to you every day. It's not a punishment; it's a support that shows faith they can turn this around.

This is a problem for just about every company with an installed CRM system. Instead of insisting on a process and creating consequences for those not using it, managers let people off the hook. It is amazing to me how a company can spend tens of thousands of dollars that will only help the best salespeople to get better and work smarter and then never hold them accountable for using it. In this situation, you must switch back to a supervisor role and make compliance mandatory.

DISC (DOMINANT, INFLUENCER, STEADY RELATOR, COMPLIANT)

A parallel to what we've been discussing is the DISC profile tool that Sandler uses. In DISC parlance, a high-D, also known as Dominant, would be supervisor behavior. A socially oriented high-I, also known as an Influencer, would be in line with trainer behavior. A high-S, known as a Steady Relator, would be a coach, and a high-C, known as a Complaint, would be more of a mentor who only cares about the facts. As I see it, in the call-center environment, the mentor is the person who can walk up to you and ask a single question that makes you think and gets you motivated—which means a "just the facts" attitude is a good match here. So the big question is, can you be good enough to change your roles and grow your people?

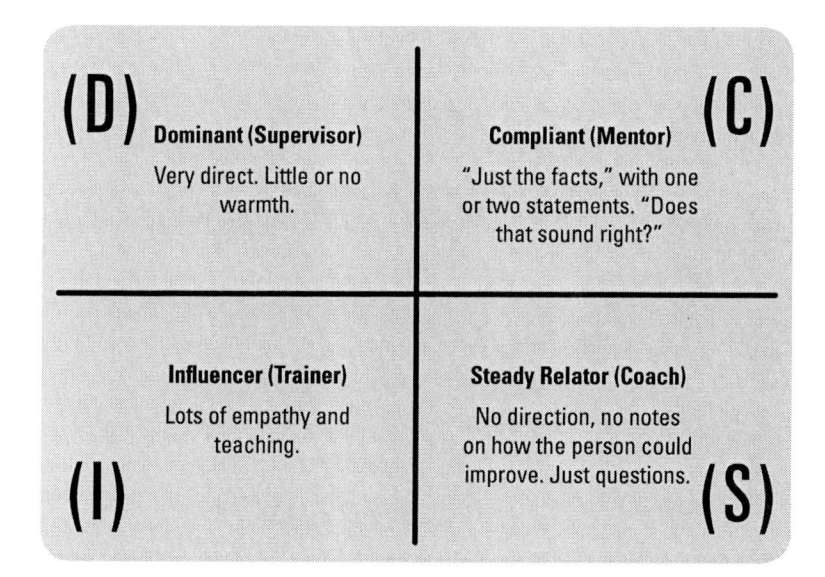

(D) Dominant (Supervisor) Very direct. Little or no warmth.	**Compliant (Mentor) (C)** "Just the facts," with one or two statements. "Does that sound right?"
Influencer (Trainer) Lots of empathy and teaching. **(I)**	**Steady Relator (Coach)** No direction, no notes on how the person could improve. Just questions. **(S)**

Once you know your own DISC profile, it will be easier for you to figure out which of the above approaches comes easiest to you—and which adaptations are in order so you can fulfill all four roles seamlessly, as the situation warrants.

Now, let's take a look at how the Sandler sales management principles play out in the real world—in a busy call center.

TO SUM UP: You have four different but complementary jobs as the manager of a call center: supervisor, trainer, coach, and mentor. The deeper your understanding of the four DISC behavioral styles, the more effective you will be at doing those four different jobs.

CHAPTER TWELVE

A Deeper Dive into Managing a Call Center

Now that you've got a sense of the depth and complexity of the sales manager's job—now that you understand this is a job with more levels and deeper responsibilities than most people realize—you're in a good position to move on to the next critical stage of understanding and practice. You're ready to look more closely at how intelligent sales management can (and, I believe, should) maximize performance in a call center.

In the most successful call centers, the transition from supervisor to mentor happens quite rapidly. The reason for this is that the productive call center itself works at a much faster pace than a call center that posts only mediocre numbers. While an average outside-selling salesperson might make 25 calls a day, in a successful call center, salespeople are making and/or taking between 150 and 250 calls a day.

That's a lot of calls! Among other things, that heavy call volume—which is both healthy and sustainable—means that the transition to initial competency that typically takes representatives a matter of months can and should take place in a matter of weeks or even days—if the sales managers know what they are doing.

If you are willing to commit to being that kind of sales manager, my first piece of advice to you is simple: Be ready, willing, and able to move from supervisor to coach with each and every one of your new hires individually and at a much faster pace than you are doing so currently. I typically recommend two to four weeks, a target that startles a lot of people. I set this goal with my clients for two reasons.

- **Reason #1:** The cost to the company of making that phone ring is high. For most of us, the cost is just too expensive to justify someone taking the usual three calendar months' worth of calls to learn the ropes.
- **Reason #2:** The cost of employee turnover is high, too—and not just in dollars. Whenever someone opts to leave your team, that decision has an adverse effect on morale for everyone. You want to narrow the window within which that decision typically takes place.

Transitioning people from a "new hire" state of mind to an "I belong here" state of mind in 10–30 calendar days, rather than 30–90 calendar days, will reduce your overall churn rate and—perhaps just as important—increase retention among your top performers.

This is a fast-paced world in which you are asking people to succeed. Anything you do to reduce turnover makes it easier for people to conclude they've picked the right team. Anything that increases turnover makes it easy for people to get discouraged. Once they're discouraged, that all-important enthusiastic attitude can go south quickly, with consequences for the entire team. Attitude problems in a call center tend to correlate with high turnover numbers, and tend be highly contagious. Just a couple of bad phone calls from one person can snowball. Before you know it, that one person whose best friend just left the call center is having a negative impact on everyone's productivity.

Call-center sales managers ignore the issues I have raised here at their own peril. Growth within the position must happen quickly.

SUPERVISING: BEFORE THE PERSON GETS ON THE PHONE

I tell my clients that the supervisor part of the sales manager's role should be one of sharing what already works, not asking new hires to improvise. Everything the new hire should do and say must be clearly explained and outlined on the very first day, and the new hire must be held to a high mark for executing, as instructed, starting with the very first call. In other words (to give the most obvious and probably most important example), when new hires start, they should be following a script that is already written. This script should be memorized before hires are allowed on the phone.

That requirement comes as a surprise to a lot of our new clients, but we consider it non-negotiable in the call-center environment. In fact, the new hire must not only have memorized the script before being allowed to get on the phone but also be able to repeat the script word for word in several different speeds and tones. Getting the new hire to this point of readiness is one of the supervisor's most important jobs.

Very often, when we work with a call center, we develop not only the script's words, but also the script's flowchart, with the most likely possible outcomes of each question and clear instructions on which direction a given response should take the sales call.

A Deeper Dive into Managing a Call Center

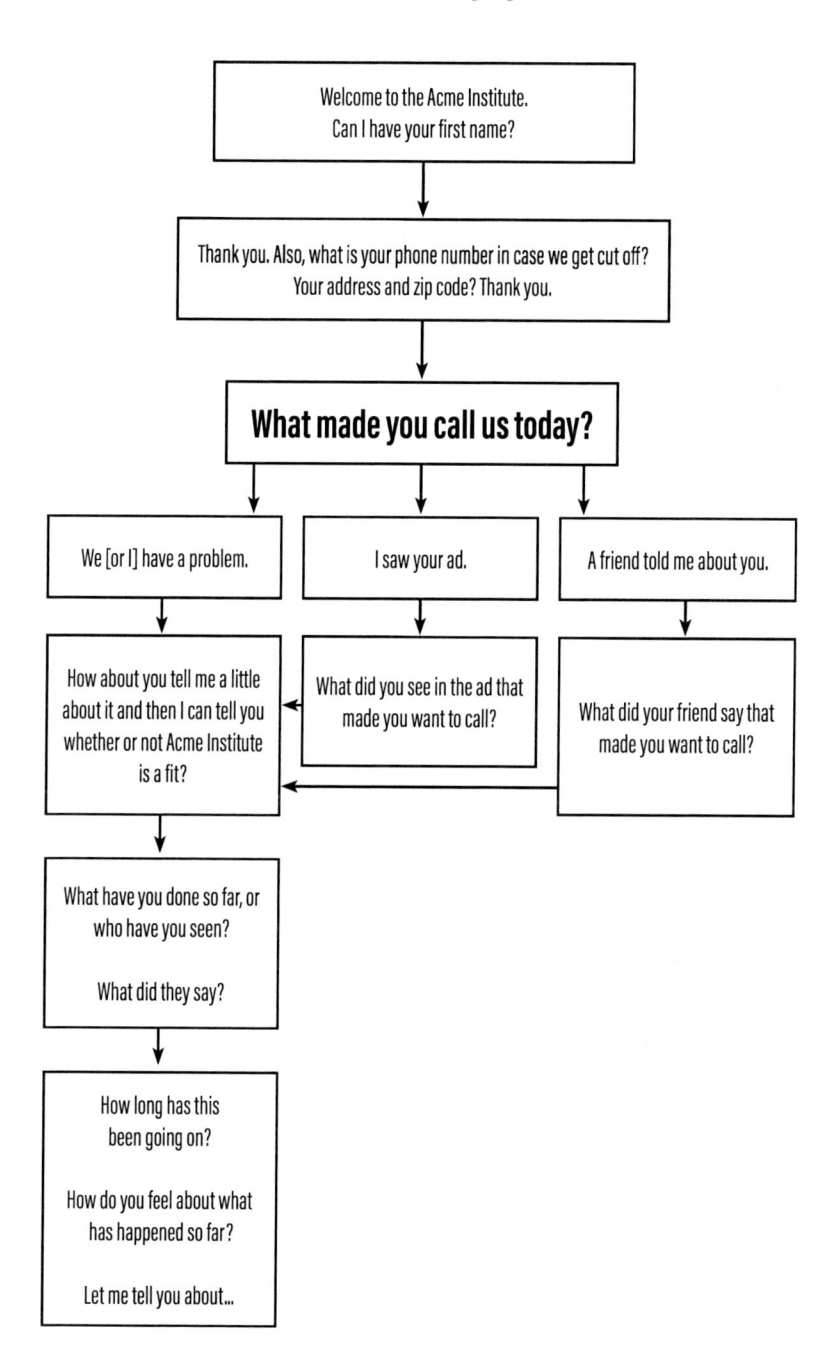

```
┌─────────────────────────────────┐
│    Welcome to the Acme Institute.│
│    Can I have your first name?   │
└─────────────────────────────────┘
                │
                ▼
┌─────────────────────────────────────────────────┐
│ Thank you. Also, what is your phone number in   │
│ case we get cut off?                            │
│ Your address and zip code? Thank you.           │
└─────────────────────────────────────────────────┘
                │
                ▼
    **What made you call us today?**
        │         │         │
        ▼         ▼         ▼
 ┌──────────┐ ┌──────────┐ ┌──────────────────┐
 │ We [or I]│ │ I saw    │ │ A friend told me │
 │ have a   │ │ your ad. │ │ about you.       │
 │ problem. │ │          │ │                  │
 └──────────┘ └──────────┘ └──────────────────┘
        │         │              │
        ▼         ▼              ▼
 ┌──────────────┐ ┌──────────────┐ ┌──────────────────┐
 │ How about you│ │ What did you │ │ What did your    │
 │ tell me a    │◄│ see in the ad│ │ friend say that  │
 │ little about │ │ that made you│ │ made you want    │
 │ it and then I│ │ want to call?│ │ to call?         │
 │ can tell you │ └──────────────┘ └──────────────────┘
 │ whether or   │                          │
 │ not Acme     │◄─────────────────────────┘
 │ Institute    │
 │ is a fit?    │
 └──────────────┘
        │
        ▼
 ┌──────────────────────────────┐
 │ What have you done so far, or│
 │ who have you seen?           │
 │                              │
 │ What did they say?           │
 └──────────────────────────────┘
        │
        ▼
 ┌──────────────────────────────┐
 │ How long has this            │
 │ been going on?               │
 │                              │
 │ How do you feel about what   │
 │ has happened so far?         │
 │                              │
 │ Let me tell you about...     │
 └──────────────────────────────┘
```

If this is not done, you will waste precious time and money—and you will have a high turnover rate. Once everyone is working from the same script and the same flowchart, you're in a position to coach them and get their best performance.

COACHING: TEAM DISCUSSIONS

There are many coaching opportunities with your people each day.

The first opportunity should be in a group setting. You might start out a sales meeting with the replay of an audio recording of a good sales call from the day before. (Make sure you follow all relevant legal guidelines for recording such conversations.) After you finish playing the call for the group, simply ask the group these questions and guide the discussion that follows each.

- What went right with that call?
- Is there anything you think the salesperson should have done differently?
- How could the salesperson have changed the outcome?

Then you pick out a less effective sales call, play that for the group, and ask:

- What went right with that call?
- What should the salesperson have done differently?
- How could the salesperson have changed the outcome?

Unless you are in training mode (which comes next in the sequence), this is a great place for your people to learn from their peers. You just facilitate the discussion. You will be amazed how well your people can debrief the calls and help each other out.

Then have everyone stand up and do your daily huddle. Go around the room and ask two, and only two, questions of everyone, questions that focus on something you are interested in measuring. Tell the group you only want the numbers and supporting statements in one sentence or less—nothing else.

Your questions might be:

- How many calls are you going to make today?
- What will you do differently today than you did yesterday, and how will you measure that?

This two-question huddle is meant to build energy and get everyone focused on the most important things: behavior and growth.

COACHING: ONE-ON-ONE DISCUSSIONS

Now let's take a look at one-on-one coaching in the call-center environment. You should set aside time for everyone on the staff for one-on-one discussions. How often this happens depends on the size of the sales force, but optimally you should have a weekly one-on-one discussion with each employee. There are three important rules of the road you will need to follow when it comes to holding these sessions.

1. **The sessions should be consistent.** In other words, if you're doing them weekly, they need to occur at the same time and on the same day of the week for each person. A manager might block out all day on Friday for one-on-ones, for instance, and make sure the meetings show up on each employee's calendar.
2. **The sales representatives must be protected.** In the meetings, there must be no attacks nor anything that could even be perceived as an attack. You get to ask questions, but you don't get to say, "Here's how I would have done it," or "You made a mistake when you…" You must remain coach only. That means you are only allowed to ask questions during the meeting. No statements! If you make statements, you are either training or you are supervising. This is a coaching session.
3. **Coaching is not about telling people what to do.** It's about asking good questions and encouraging people to come to their own conclusions about what to do next.

That's coaching. If you feel the need to have a different type of meeting, then set up a different meeting. Don't do it here. The coaching one-on-one meetings must be a protected environment if you want people to open up to you. That's your job as a coach—to get them to open up.

An example of a good coaching session might sound something like this:

The manager opens the meeting by setting the agenda in a way the salesperson can and does buy into.

Manager: How are you doing these days? [Or a similar bonding question, asked with genuine concern.]

Salesperson: [Any response. Manager listens, responds appropriately.]

Manager: Can we go over your call numbers?

Salesperson: Sure.

Manager: How did the numbers yesterday look to you?

Salesperson: They're lower than the targets I'm supposed to hit.

Manager: OK, what will you do next week to get your numbers up?

Salesperson: I'm going to focus more on doing a better job of identifying people who are just wasting my time.

Manager: How will that make a difference?

Salesperson: I find I tend to get into conversations with people who just want to talk, especially when I have had a bad day of not connecting to people. It makes me feel better sometimes to talk to anyone. So I want to change that pattern.

Manager: Great. Now let's take a look at your last week's calls. Can you tell me about a good call and why you thought it was good?

Salesperson: I talked to this one person and she... [etc.]

Manager: OK. What could you have done differently to get a different, even better outcome?

Salesperson: I could have... [etc.]

Manager: What else?

Salesperson: Hmm. I could have... [etc.]

Manager: Now let's talk about a call that didn't go well. What happened?

Salesperson: I talked to this one person and he... [etc.]

Manager: What could you have done differently to get a different outcome in that situation?

Salesperson: Let's see. I could have... [etc.]

Manager: And what else?

Salesperson: I guess I could have... [etc.]

As you can see the whole purpose of this is self-learning and self-discovery. Your salespeople will grow and change much faster if they come up with their own solutions, rather than hear them from your mouth.

Of course, during this conversation you might see spots for further training. At that point, you might say, "I think we should set aside some time for you to get better trained on that."

You might even note that they are not doing what you ask them three or four times in a row. Then, you might set up a supervisor meeting. What you say could sound like this: "I think we are done with our coaching session today—but I need you to meet with me before you go home for a heart-to-heart discussion."

ONSITE COACHING

In a call center, there are plenty of opportunities for what I call "onsite coaching." This is where you sit with someone and listen to him during a sales call. Then, right after the call, you go over it in detail, using the same questions from a one-on-one coaching session. This is analogous to the "ride along" for outside-selling salespeople. With today's technology, this has become pretty easy. You can now hit a button and listen in on another conversation. In fact, you can get systems that allow you to talk to the salesperson without letting the person on the other end of the phone hear you.

We have a rule during these sessions: When the manager says something in your ear, it must come out of your mouth. Consider the cost of leads. Every time you have a connection, the quicker you turn those rings into dollars instead of into dial tones, the better. By the way, what role are you playing when you do that? Supervisor!

What role are you playing the minute you hang up the phone? Coach. That's the time to ask questions: "Why do you think I said that?" "Why do you think it's difficult for you to say that?" "What would have happened if…?" And so on.

In a call center you must be able to jump from supervisor to coach at a moment's notice.

Once again you can't do any of these well if you haven't let the supervisor out and created the sales processes and the metrics you will use in your sales process.

So go to work and build the process.

TRAINING

We talked before about why the supervisor's role is so important. Supervising is where you lay the process and the scripts out clearly. Of course, effective training is part of that. But training can and does happen after the initial ramp-up period as well. Maybe something got skipped or was forgotten. Maybe there's a new script to learn. If you don't have a process, you really can't train—you can only talk.

The reason Sandler has created a strong process is so that it can be trained and reinforced over time. In a call center, managers as trainers use their knowledge of the system not to catch people doing something wrong, but to help them refine each step with which they are having trouble.

Too often people think that the trainer is a coach, but there is an important difference. The trainer tells people how to execute a certain skill, while a coach only asks questions.

A call-center trainer is good at switching roles in the moment. In other words, while walking the floor the manager is listening for those training moments. When the person hangs up the phone, the manager can step right in and say, "Let's role-play what just happened."

In good call-center training role-plays, the manager becomes the salesperson and the salesperson gets to be the prospect. The salesperson can then see how the manager would have used the Sandler system to take the call to a different outcome.

A good call-center manager is always looking for opportunities to go into training mode while on the floor.

MENTORING

The role of a mentor is reserved for interactions with those employees who want to use the process and the data to improve constantly. Being a good mentor means saying, in essence, "I don't have to train or coach you, but here's a simple comment that can help you to improve or to go in a different direction." The mentor discussion is different from the coaching discussion in the call-center environment because: a) it tends to focus on a single pointed observation or question, and b) it tends to come along at a moment when the employee is not expecting it. Not everyone on your team is ready for a mentor.

Think of mentors in your own past. Haven't you had a mentor, if not in your parents, in someone you respected, who would say something like, "Did that make sense to you when you did it?" and then walk away? This has the effect of making you think about how else you could have done it rather than solving it for you. This is why you will only be mentoring a few people at a time.

Note: When people you are mentoring go into a slump or something happens to them and their numbers dip, you can't stay in that role. You must move back to supervising temporarily. When this happens, expect pushback from them. You might hear things like, "I have been here four years—I shouldn't be treated like this." That is when you say, "You are right. But you are my best performer, and you are off track. I will manage the heck out of you until you are back on track."

In the next chapter, I'll share some thoughts on hiring.

> **TO SUM UP:** In this chapter, you learned more about the four jobs of the sales manager: supervisor, coach, trainer, and mentor.

CHAPTER THIRTEEN

Hiring the Right Salespeople for Your Call Center

I've already mentioned that comparatively high turnover of salespeople is a fact of life in the call-center environment. This is a reality of the industry, and there's not a lot you can do to change that. With that reality in mind, we come to the next big question: What steps can you take to ensure that you hire the right people in the first place—and minimize the impact those high turnover numbers have on performance?

A DIFFERENT BREED

First of all, you have to understand that successful call-center salespeople are different than other salespeople. You can't expect to hire them the same way you would hire field salespeople, and you can't expect them to take the same approach to the job that a field salesperson would.

Specifically, the temperament and personality of a successful call-center salesperson is likely to be very different from that of a successful field salesperson. As a general but reliable rule, you are looking for people who like to be alone and prefer not to be in front of people all the time. You are looking for people who shun the spotlight. That's totally different from the typical high-achieving field salesperson. Those folks usually love to be around others, and they are likely to be very comfortable indeed at center stage.

You need to understand, too, that a call-center salesperson doesn't look at the job in the same way a field salesperson does—and doesn't have to. There are some things you might worry about when hiring field salespeople that you don't have to worry about when you hire a call-center representative—personal appearance, for instance.

DON'T JUDGE THE BOOK BY THE COVER

Call-center managers do have to come to terms with this issue of personal appearance. It's something that throws a lot of managers off.

Most interviewers—not just in sales, but in any number of other areas—are used to disqualifying people who come in for the meeting looking like something the cat dragged in. If you're dealing with a field sales team, that probably isn't a bad decision. Before you make that decision in a call-center environment, though, pause and consider that many of the very best call-center representatives are people who don't spend a whole lot of time socializing with others face-to-face. That means they tend to dress differently and look different than other applicants.

I don't know why that is; I don't know whether it's a positive or a negative for the people in question, and I can't pretend to explain what it says about working in a call center. But I do know that if you want to hire the very best call-center sales team, you shouldn't prejudge people on their appearance.

Accept that some people will work for you and make great contributions who look less than presentable. Some won't dress very well. Some won't be physically attractive in the classical sense. Some will have grooming issues. Some have all three of these traits. Who cares? These are qualified, motivated people looking for a way to make good money without having to leave their desk.

The moral of the story: Interview all call-center people on the phone first. Don't let your first interview be one in which you actually look at them. Appearances can be deceiving, and you don't want to be deceived. Let the person's phone identity be the first identity you encounter. Then meet face-to-face and make your best decision.

ARE THEY DRIVEN?

There are all kinds of people who make great call-center salespeople: loudmouths; very shy people; tall people; short people; smart people; not-so-smart people. But one trait they all have in common is that they are driven.

They all have personal goals that matter to them, goals to which showing up for work each day at your call center gets them closer. Some might be single parents who want to pay for their children's school and prefer a predictable schedule over the long hours of an outside-selling job. Others might be in it to add a second income that makes it easier to afford the down payment on a house. Some might want to make sure they make the monthly bills without having to rely on others for support. Still others might want to hit a certain income target without having to think too much about what they're doing: "Just tell me what to do and tell me how many calls I have to do to hit the goal. Then I'm done." Then they get to go off and have fun. That's what they're driven to make happen. That's why they show up on Monday: to earn enough money to have a really great weekend, week after week. That's fine.

Find the person who has that kind of internal motivation, and you're halfway home. So what if this individual doesn't want to get dressed up or doesn't want to have to think too hard about anything? If the person sounds good, is confident on the phone, and is coachable, you have a candidate.

ARE THEY WILLING TO MOVE?

When I talk about a person being "willing to move," no, I don't mean he should be ready to relocate to another city. Since you've made it this far in the book, it should come as no surprise to you that the people you are looking for must embrace, and fit into, a culture of nonstop physical movement. Standing up and sitting down has to be part of this job. You don't want to hire someone who expects to make calls hunched over in a little corner, cut off from the rest of the group.

As I've already made clear, the physical workspace itself must radiate movement and energy. There should be a sense of shared, dynamic group space, not static individual cubicles. Your people should stand up whenever they are engaged in a discussion with a prospect. Guess what? Someone you are interviewing in person for a sales position should be able to see this movement happening in the call center—instantly.

That means you must have a strong call-center culture, a culture that's based on physical movement. That culture must be so deeply ingrained that people who come in to interview for a job with you know right away, the minute they see the room where people make calls, that they will either love working for you or hate it from day one.

Wouldn't you both rather know which it is—right away?

This is yet another reason why room setup and the way

management interacts with the team is important. Creating a strong culture is a critical part of attracting the right people.

> **TO SUM UP:** The temperament and personality of a successful call-center salesperson is likely to be very different from that of a successful field salesperson, and your hiring decisions should reflect that fact.

THE SCRIPTS

CHAPTER FOURTEEN

The Scripts

You have the right people, the right environment, and the right management. Now you need the right words.

Here's a brief recap of the opening phases of the Sandler Selling System. It will help you to make sense of the model scripts I'm sharing below, which use these three steps as their foundation.

Step 1. Build rapport. This, you'll recall, means real rapport, as opposed to fake rapport. Everyone has been on the receiving end of fake rapport. It's when you walk into a store or car dealership and the first words out of a salesperson's mouth are something like, "Wow, that's a nice shirt." What happens next? Admit it. You think, "Oh no—a salesperson." That's not what this step is all about. Real rapport creates an environment where two people can talk on an equal Adult-to-Adult level. It could start with something like, "I'm looking for a little help—I'm not even sure we should be talking." Or, "My timing may be way off and if it is let me know..." The real goal is to start the conversation off on the right foot.

Step 2. Set an up-front contract. As you know, this step sets the expectation for what is going to happen on the call in terms of time, agenda, and possible outcomes. In a call center, it could sound like this: "Can I take 30 seconds and tell you why I called, and you can tell me if you want more information or if I should go away?"

Step 3. Uncover pain. The goal here is to find out how doing things the way the prospect is currently doing them is hurting the prospect. Uncovering pain, as we've shown, means identifying the emotional gap between where the person is now and where he wants to be. There is very little time for this on the phone so the key is to create pain statements that will hook the prospect into wanting more information. This is not done in the traditional "try to tell the prospect everything you possibly can before he hangs up," but by driving a two-way conversation. The only way to do this is to develop meaningful questions to get prospects to interact with your salespeople. These must be prepared ahead of time. Following is a chart that can help you create pain questions.

What do we sell?	What do they really buy?	What is the emotion behind why they buy?	Hot button
Life insurance	Security	Fear	No worries for anyone about the future
Credit collections service	A faster return on their money	Frustration	Shrink their daily sales outstanding

And here's a blank form you can use to create the questions yourself.

What do we sell?	What do they really buy?	What is the emotion behind why they buy?	Hot button

Now let's put a script together using these principles.

Example #1, Outbound (Seeking a Second Phone Appointment for a Multi-Call Sale)

Rapport/Pattern Interrupt: Maria, Tom Niesen. Maria, I am looking for a little help. I'm not sure if it makes sense for us to speak.

Mini Up-Front-Contract: Let me tell you the reason why I am calling and then we can decide together if it makes sense to keep talking. Is that fair?

Make a Personal Connection (Optional): I saw the story about your company in the *Dallas Business Times* on your expansion.

—or—

I see that we both know Isaac Hero.

—or—

I understand that we both belong to the Dallas Chamber of Commerce.

10-Second Mini-Commercial: I work with ABC Company. We are a credit-collection firm. I spend my time with presidents and owners of companies.

Fish for Pain (Stroke, Pain, Impact): Maria, when I speak to owners, here is what they often tell me.

Stroke: They have a good accounts-receivable department doing a great job...

Pain: ...but they are occasionally frustrated that something falls through the cracks in collections...

Impact: ...and they are finding it hurts the monthly numbers.

Stroke: Other times, it is not the one or two accounts that's the issue...

Pain: ...it seems their daily sales outstanding is getting longer and longer...

Impact: ...and that is hurting their cash flow overall.

Stroke: Other times their DSO is fine...

Pain: ...but there is one good account that they want their money from faster but they don't want to lose the account in the process...

Impact: ...and this impacts their margins.

Hook Question: Maria, I don't want to make any assumptions. Have any of these things ever been an issue for you? Is it worth a short conversation?

Global Pain Questions (Issue, Example, Impact): Can you tell me more? Can you give me a recent real life example? Because of this, what happened?

Close for the Appointment: Maria, can I make a suggestion? Take a look at your calendar and let's find an hour or so in the next few weeks when we can set up a longer time to talk by phone.

The Up-Front Contract: I can take a little more time to understand a bit more about [pain issue revealed above]. You can have the opportunity to pick my brain and learn more about other organizations that may have had similar issues. At the end, you and I can decide if it makes sense to invest more time together. If not, no problem. It's just two business people in Dallas who have had a chance to talk. No harm, no foul. Our services certainly aren't for everybody. If you and I think it makes sense to build a relationship and find a way to work together, we can make out the plan at the end of our time together. Does that sound fair? Pick a day.

Homework: Do one more thing for me, please. If you can, give some thought before we talk as to what the three or four sales issues are that your organization faces that can be a good place to start the discussion. Maria, I will talk to you at [date, time], and I will call this number. What is your email address so I can send you a meeting invitation?

Example #2, Includes Post-Sell

Pattern Interrupt: Derek, Tom Niesen. Derek, I am looking for a little help. I'm not sure if it makes sense for us to speak.

Mini Up-Front Contract: Let me tell you the reason why I am calling and then we can decide together if it makes sense to keep talking. Is that fair?

Make a Personal Connection (Optional): I saw the story about your company in the *Dallas Business Times* on your expansion.

—or—

I see that we both know Isaac Hero.

—or—

I understand that we both belong to the Dallas Chamber of Commerce.

10-Second Mini-Commercial: I work with Acuity Systems and Sandler Training. We are a sales training and sales force development company. I spend my time with presidents and owners of IT organizations [or whatever industry].

Fish for Pain (Stroke, Pain, Impact): Derek, when I speak to owners, here is what they often tell me.

Stroke: They have a senior sales force that is good at what they do and excellent products...

Pain: ...but they are occasionally frustrated that their people have proposed a fair amount of business and for whatever reason it does not seem to be closing...

Impact: ...and they are finding that their forecasts get busted and they are missing budgets.

Stroke: Other times, it is not the pipeline that's the issue...

Pain: ...but they just do not seem to be bringing enough new business in on a consistent enough basis...

Impact: ...to grow the way they as owners want to grow.

Stroke: Other times, they can bring in new accounts...

Pain: ...but find the marketplace wants to commoditize their offerings and they find themselves discounting aggressively to win the business...

Impact: ...and this impacts their margins.

Hook Question: Derek, I don't want to make any assumptions. Have any of these things ever been an issue for you? Is it worth a short conversation?

Global Pain Questions (Issue, Example, Impact): Can you tell me more? Can you give me a recent real life example? Because of this, what happened?

Close for the Appointment: Derek, can I make a suggestion? Take a look at your calendar and let's find an hour or so in the next few weeks where we can set up a longer time to talk by phone.

The Up-Front Contract: I can take a little more time to understand a bit more about [pain revealed above]. You can have the opportunity to pick my brain and learn a little more about other organizations that may have had similar issues. At the end then, you and I can decide if it makes sense to invest more time together. If not, no problem. It's just two business people in Dallas who have had a chance to talk. No harm, no foul. Our company's services certainly aren't for everybody. If you and I think it makes sense to build a relationship and find a way to work together, we can make out the plan at the end of our time together. Sound fair? Pick a day.

Post-Sell: I have you down for [date, time]. I am looking at my calendar. It doesn't look like I am going to have time to check voicemails or emails that morning. Is there any reason at all that you see now that would cause you to have to change, cancel, or reschedule for any reason? Great.

Homework: Do one more thing for me, please. If you can, give some thought as to what the three or four sales issues are that your organization faces that can be a good place to start the discussion. Derek, I will talk to you at [time] on [date], and I will call you at [number]. What is your email address, Derek, so I can send you a meeting invitation?

Example #3, Inbound

Pattern Interrupt: Hello. This is Tom. Thank you so much for calling, Chris.

Mini Up-Front Contract: Can you tell me the reason for

your call, and then I will take 30 seconds to tell you about us and you can decide if you want more information?

Make a Personal Connection (Optional): I have heard about your company...

–*or*–

I see you are calling from...

–*or*–

I understand that we both belong to the Dallas Chamber of Commerce...

10-Second Mini-Commercial: I work with AX. We are a data-collection software company for the rental industry. I spend my time with other analysts like yourself.

Fish for Pain (Stroke, Pain, Impact): Chris, when I speak to analysts who are looking for information...

Stroke: ...I find they have a good way to get some of the data they need to make rental decisions...

Pain: ...but they are occasionally frustrated that the market changes faster than their data shows...

Impact: ...and that that hurts their overall numbers.

Stroke: Other times, it is not their rental data they are looking for...

Pain: ...but they are trying to make informed decisions about buying new property...

Impact: ...so they don't miss a good investment opportunity to grow their portfolio.

Stroke: Other times...

Pain: ...it is not buying but selling at the right time for which they need the data.

Impact: Otherwise their margins get impacted.

Hook Question: Chris, I don't want to make any assumptions. Have any of these things ever been an issue for you? Is it worth a short conversation?

Global Pain Questions (Issue, Example, Impact): Can you tell me more? Can you give me a recent real life example? Because of this, what happened?

Close for the Appointment: Chris, can I make a suggestion? Take a look at your calendar and let's find a time to set up a one-hour webinar where I can walk you through how our system works.

DEVELOP YOUR OWN

Now you try. On the following pages is a template. What does your script look like? Once you've developed it, how can you analyze it, test it, and improve it?

Pattern Interrupt:

_____

_____

Mini Up-Front Contract:

_____

_____

Make a Personal Connection (Optional):

_____

_____

10-Second Mini-Commercial:

_____

_____

Fish for Pain (Stroke, Pain, Impact):

_____

_____

Stroke:

_____

_____

Pain:

_____

_____

Impact:

_____

_____

Stroke:

_____

_____

Pain:

_____

_____

Impact:

_____

_____

Stroke:

_____

_____

Pain:

_____

_____

Impact:

_____

_____

Hook Question:

_____

_____

Global Pain Questions (Issue, Example, Impact): Can you tell me more? Can you give me a recent real life example? Because of this, what happened?

_____

_____

Close for the Appointment:
_____

_____

The Up-Front Contract:
_____

_____

Post-Sell:
_____

_____

Homework:
_____

_____

ONCE YOU HAVE THE RIGHT SCRIPT—FOLLOW IT!

Here is the big thing about scripts. Once you have them down, new hires (and everyone else) must follow them. As a matter of fact, when we work with a call center, within the first week we make sure that each and every employee is able to role-play that script in several different tones of voice and at several different speeds.

Once you have a script and you have tracked its success, executing it as written becomes your employees' must-do if they want to keep their jobs. The company spends a lot of money to make that phone ring, and salespeople should know that they only have one shot at a sale when they answer the phone. You don't want employees shooting from the hip—you want them sticking with what works. Once you know you have a script that works, make it part of your team culture to use it as it's laid out. That's the behavior that matters in the call-center environment: executing the script.

I'll close this chapter with some of the best advice David Sandler ever shared. It's advice that is particularly relevant to salespeople who are aiming to succeed in this kind of selling, advice I hope you will share with your team on a regular basis:

Do the behaviors!
Do the behaviors!
Do the behaviors!

> **TO SUM UP:** In this chapter, you studied sample scripts and a script development template. Use them—then test and refine the resulting scripts you create for your team.

THE ROAD FROM HERE

EPILOGUE

By teaching clients how to put the principles in this book to work, we've helped countless organizations move from the stereotypical "boiler room" mentality that too many still associate with call centers to a professional inside-selling mentality—with profits to match. But we've also found that just knowing what to do isn't enough. When it comes to transforming the physical layout and the culture of a call center, it is likely that you will need not just sound tactics but also effective training, supervision, mentoring, and coaching—so that you as the manager can offer all four of those elements to your team.

If you'd like some help implementing and reinforcing the ideas you've read about here, please visit us at Sandler.com—so you can reach out to your local Sandler trainer.

APPENDIX: CASE STUDY

Note: The company in the following case study used a powerful Sandler strategy for securing team "buy-in" on the concept of setting and recording daily performance metrics. Team members who failed to keep track of their own behavioral numbers were charged a 20% fine on their monthly commissions. It didn't take long for call-center representatives to "get religion" on the importance of monitoring and recording their daily performance totals.

CASE STUDY

PCI

Sandler Tools and Processes Raise Call-Center Revenue per Hour by 100%

BUSINESS CHALLENGE

Dallas-based PCI helps college, university, and association clients engage their alumni and membership and raise money so that they can fulfill their mission of educating America's future leaders. The company partners with its clients to collect massive amounts of data from their alumni membership, publish alumni and membership directories, create and manage dynamic online communities, and implement innovative fundraising programs.

When PCI began working with Sandler, the business challenges were to:

- Create a "wow" experience with every sales call.
- Improve morale.
- Increase call-center revenue per hour.

"We reached out to Sandler because we wanted to establish a much more structured approach to our call center for alumni directory sales," recalls Tom Lyons, PCI's COO. "We wanted to improve the caller's experience, deliver a deeper level of job satisfaction to the members of the team, and see some major changes in the sales metrics we were getting. Sandler helped us set up a long-term plan for accomplishing those things."

SANDLER SOLUTIONS

Lyons and his Sandler trainer took a close look at PCI's call-center operations—and decided to embark on a major makeover. This included:

- Training and reinforcing key Sandler concepts with members of the call-center team.
- Creating customized calling scripts and communication protocols based on the Sandler Selling System.
- Creating a "cookbook" (daily behavior plan) for each call-center representative and holding each representative

accountable for meeting or exceeding his behavior targets.
- Familiarizing each call-center representative with the DISC behavioral model—and sharing and reinforcing best practices for adapting to a prospect's DISC style.
- Completely redesigning the physical call center, in accordance with Sandler's revolutionary "open workspace" strategy for call centers.

All five of these action items were important, but Lyons calls particular attention to the last one as a sign of Sandler's and PCI's joint commitment to change the work environment. "We gutted the old call-center area," he recalls. "We took down the walls and cubicles, remodeled everything, and opened it all up, as our Sandler trainer recommended. Now everyone could see everyone else—and also see everyone else's results in real time, thanks to the big display monitors. It was a totally different environment, a totally different workplace dynamic."

Working in concert with other management initiatives (notably a change in compensation and recruitment plans), Sandler delivered dramatic positive outcomes for PCI. They're summarized below.

RESULTS

- Per person revenue per hour figures increased from under $50 to over $100–and stayed there.

- Employee morale is high.
- *Texas Monthly Magazine* named PCI the #1 mid-sized company to work for in the state of Texas.

"We didn't deliver those results overnight, and doing so wasn't cheap," Lyons says now, "but our partnership with Sandler made a major positive impact in the long term. It allowed us to change the employee experience for the better, change the customer experience for the better, and post some remarkable, sustainable improvements in our sales numbers. Sandler's consulting, its delivery on its commitments, and its long-term reinforcement of key learning concepts were game-changers. Our decision to work with Sandler was an excellent investment."

ABOUT THE COMPANY

PCI is a Texas-based company that utilizes technology, expertise, best practices, and proven products and services to help colleges, universities, independent schools, fraternities, sororities, and associations of all types drive engagement and maximize contributions.

Company Website: publishingconcepts.com

For more information about Sandler Training, visit www.sandler.com.

Look for these other books
on shop.sandler.com:

Prospect the Sandler Way

Transforming Leaders the Sandler Way

Selling Professional Services the Sandler Way

Accountability the Sandler Way

Selling Technology the Sandler Way

LinkedIn the Sandler Way

Bootstrap Selling the Sandler Way

Customer Service the Sandler Way

Selling to Homeowners the Sandler Way

Succeed the Sandler Way

The Contrarian Salesperson

The Sales Coach's Playbook

Lead When You Dance

Change the Sandler Way

Motivational Management the Sandler Way

CRASH A CLASS AND EXPERIENCE THE
POWER OF SANDLER
YOU HAVE NOTHING TO LOSE AND EVERYTHING TO GAIN.

Are you a **salesperson** who...

- Feels uneasy about the lack of qualified prospects in your pipeline?
- Spends too much time developing proposals that do not turn into business?
- Wastes time with unqualified prospects?
- Continues to get 'think-it-overs' instead of closing?

Are you a **sales leader** who...

- Is frustrated with managing a sales force that's not meeting goals?
- Is tired of hiring salespeople that won't prospect?

Expand your reach and success by attending a complimentary training session at a local Sandler office near you.

REASONS TO
CRASH A CLASS

- Improve your current processes.
- Go "beyond the book" and witness an interactive, in-person approach to a small group training.
- Discover a workable, ground-level solution.

Contact a Sandler trainer to reserve your seat today.
www.sandler.com/CRASH-A-CLASS